BLOOD TRAILS
ACROSS TEXAS

Blood Trails Across Texas

ISBN: 978-0-9837073-6-3

Black Dog Swamp Publishing Co.
PO Box 3365
Early, Texas 76803

www.texastruecrime.com

BLOOD TRAILS ACROSS TEXAS

By Brian R. Foster
Houston Homicide (Ret)

Book One of the Texas True Crime Series

Other books by Brian R. Foster

Homicidal Humor
More Homicidal Humor
The Clot Thickens

•TABLE OF CONTENTS•

•RECOGNITION AND THANKS•

I want to thank the following people for their input and help getting source material for this book. There are a couple of folks who did not want to be mentioned by name. I will not rat you out but still want you to know I appreciate your contributions.

Alfred Herrmann
Frank Scoggins and Jim Scoggins
Trampas Gooding
Rico Garcia
Scott Dobyanski
Harry Womack
Ted Wilson and Doug Osterberg
Jim Boy
David Calhoun
Mike Peters
Ismael F. "Iffy" Flores and John Parker
Al Cuellar
James Foster
Mike Williams and Lee Dawson
Steven Murdock
Charles Westbrook
Anyone I Failed to List

•DEDICATION•

This book is dedicated to the memory of two good cops. Their names were David Collier and Larry Ott. Both worked as Houston Homicide investigators. They were not showboats or hotdogs, just hard working, straightforward guys. Dave came down with lung cancer but continued working murder cases until his death. I once asked Larry why Collier did not just retire and try and enjoy the rest of the days he had on this earth. Ott responded with, "I think he wants to die a Homicide detective." Dave had thirty years I know of when he died. He was already in Homicide when I went through the police academy, and had been there a while at least. Larry Ott put in forty years with Homicide before retiring.

If I were a crook, I would want to be investigated by some pretty boy who was looking for television footage of himself or his name in print. I would fear being investigated by these two tenacious plodders who turned over every rock looking for clues, and kept at it.

•INTRODUCTION•

Scott "Doby" Dobyanski and I both worked the 4:00 p.m. to midnight shift in the Houston Police Department Homicide Division. There, we saw things your mother never told you about.

During our years in Patrol, we worked different shifts, so our paths didn't cross until we arrived in Homicide. Although we were both on the same shift in Homicide, we never worked cases together. A few years into my retirement, Doby approached me asking if I would write the story of his career case. Every cop has a career case. That case either causes them to well up with pride or its outcome sticks in their guts where it festers. Doby's career case did both. It was also a story that was too good not to be retold. While hashing out that case with him, a couple of other stories came to light (both of which are included in this book). This discussion with Doby sparked the idea of writing a series of actual homicide stories—namely, career cases—worked by officers. I have a love of short stories and began asking other retired officers from multiple locations about their career cases.

These stories span Texas from the Big Thicket to the Gulf Coast and into both the Hill Country and Big Bend Country. These investigations are the things that stuck in men's minds after a lifetime of seeing too much carnage. If any of these stories were not recorded they would be lost forever, and that would be a shame. Homicide investigation is a terribly interesting vocation, but it can eat you alive if you internalize what you see. It is also a pressure cooker of a lifestyle that comes equipped with bad coffee and political and social pressure as well. You miss too many school functions and wind up working your days off too many times. If you are lucky you don't go through too many marriages. I was once told that working Homicide was like having a very demanding mistress that you can't turn loose of and who will try and dominate your life. Therefore you need to look for a release from the madness you work in and among. I found mine by looking for humor in or around the septic tank I waded through. It helped keep me grounded. I also lived on some acreage which I looked upon as my Eden from the madhouse where I worked to pay the bills. Those guys that internalized what they saw at work developed ulcers, heart trouble, high blood pressure, suffered panic attacks, lived on happy pills or crawled up inside a bottle. Looking through a shot glass numbs you somewhat, but does not give you a clear vision of the world around or in front of you.

The names of the suspects, their co-conspirators, the victims and their family members appearing here are neither true nor correct. The victims and their families have been put through enough grief. You see, there are two categories of homicide victims. The first are the actual murder victims, and the second is the surviving loved ones. These families carry on but never really get over their loss and horror of the details.

Some of the family members in the cases I worked still keep in touch with me via the internet. Their loss never really goes away. I'm told that the pain lessens somewhat with time, but not the loss. The offspring of the murder victims are affected in ways most of us will never comprehend. Out of respect for these victims, I have changed the names and locations in these stories. I simply do not want the survivors to be contacted by curious people or reviewers of this book just because it was my opinion that the stories needed to be put into print.

In my never-to-be-humble opinion, the suspects and their co-conspirators in these cases have not suffered, and will never suffer, enough. I have not used the suspects' true names as I don't want to spend my time fending off lawsuits ginned out by one or more jake-leg lawyers. I do not want to be their next victim, and you never know when there may be a shortage of ambulances to chase. There are honorable men and women who practice law, and those I appreciate. They are the true gunfighters of their vocation. The names of persons interviewed and the people who were witnesses in these cases have similarly also been modified to protect their privacy. These modifications have also been made so several old investigators' wives can sleep better at night by not having to worry about too many things that go bump in the night.

I did, however, use the correct names of the investigating detectives and the assistant district attorneys that worked on these cases with them. They deserve the recognition for the quality of the work that was done in these matters. The convicted suspect in the first story (Robert Lumas) is now out of prison and walking the streets due to a glitch in the system. The two main suspects in "The Voodoo Queen" and "The Texas State Hotel" got what they deserved. Jones ("The Voodoo Queen") was sent directly to

Hell by the State of Texas by means of lethal injection and Turner/Kesterson ("The Texas State Hotel") got a life sentence but died from natural causes while still in prison. We like to think that his execution was carried out by a higher authority followed by his real and eternal judgment day.

Before we get into the meat of these investigations I'd like to plant a seed or two in your brain about some things you may never have been exposed to. Bear with me a moment and you may well come away with a bit of an education into the darker side of man.

Psychos, Wackos, and Things to Ponder Upon

I have been a student of human nature all of my life and really found my niche while working in Houston's Homicide Division. By working homicides you get a look into the private and most human sides of life. Some victims are the true innocents, while others have a side of their life they have actively sought to hide.

Regarding the criminals you seek as a criminal investigator, social scientists kick around the terms *sociopath* and *psychopath* a lot. Just think of a sociopath as someone who is without morals, and is a totally self-centered, manipulative brat. Their character traits blend with those of the criminal psychopath. These deviants are rarely successful and tend to be sporadic in their lives and behavior. Both groups have two primary words in their vocabularies: *I* and *me*. The psychopath is an individual that may or may not be criminally oriented—and will typically have one constant trait that is always present and which makes him what he truly is. Again, he may share all or some of the traits of the sociopath.

The thing that has interested me over the years is that when they get into trouble, these scholars will most often turn to a woman for help. They can beat their women, rob and kill people with no remorse, but when not in control they will run straight to a mother, grandmother, girlfriend, aunt, or sister. This monster may laugh as he cuts someone's heart out with a dull knife but then cry "Momma, Momma, Momma" as soon as he gets caught.

The psychopath is completely unable to internalize guilt. There are many other personality traits that are usually present in this group, and just how strongly those other traits are expressed, and which facets dominate the individual determine what that person's personality is going to be. This individual is a risk taker and will be impulsive.

Very few true psychopaths are women. I have known only one such person and she was both well organized and intelligent. In fact, she had a PhD in geophysics. I did not make her official diagnosis, but the Texas Department of Criminal Justice did during her two prison terms. In fact, she handled her own successful appeal in the attempted murder of her estranged second husband's girlfriend. While out on an appeal bond she stalked her ex-husband and his current wife while wearing disguises. During her appeal process her second former husband's house was burned down by an unknown arsonist. Her second case was retried and she was convicted once more. Her first arrest was for the shooting of her first husband (in the buttocks) in a Houston airport parking lot. She got probation in that case. Her second prison stay was for a stalking case I filed. She was caught on video multiple times and pled guilty. She served both of her prison terms completely as she did not want supervision upon release.

The intelligence levels among most psychopaths are usually (thankfully) only moderate. Their organizational skills are poor and the personal relationships they have are shallow and often very short-lived. Any display of emotion (other than anger) is simply a learned behavior, therefore any interaction with them is about as genuine as a conversation with a Myna bird.

In other words, the psychopath is a chameleon. These people (psychos and sociopaths), interestingly enough, are often charismatic and can be very manipulative. They are somewhat handicapped, however, in that they are unable to actually know or determine if the party they have been either lying to or are trying to manipulate really believes them or not.

If you run up on a criminally oriented psychopath with good organizational skills then society (or even worse, you) can be in store for some really serious problems. He does not need to be overly bright to succeed at attaining his twisted goals—being organized is enough. Normal people can't understand his motivation. For example, a stalker will continue their stalking of someone until that individual is no longer attractive to them. What the actual attraction is will be beyond a normal person's grasp. If he has a high IQ it can be even worse. When such an individual is not criminally oriented but intelligent they may become a captain of industry. He is not prone to give up and often has enough drive to continue trying one endeavor after another until he succeeds. He often does well in the practice of law. Fortunately for law enforcement the fact that poor organizational skills are most often exhibited by the criminal psychopath class individual is a real plus.

I am not labelling the convicted suspects in any of the following cases I have written about psychopaths or sociopaths. I have never met any of them personally and I do not have the credentials to back up such a diagnosis. I will simply let you as the reader make that decision if you so desire.

Robert Lumas (the suspect in the first story) has been filed on for multiple felony criminal charges over the course of his adult life. He has spent two hitches in prison for violent acts. Lumas was sentenced to forty years in prison for murdering a woman who had been his wife for a period of only about two whole weeks. It is my opinion (and only that) that he committed the murder because the victim had a little over three hundred thousand dollars in life insurance. She fortunately did not make him her beneficiary of those policies before she was murdered. He only served ten calendar years for that crime. This is probably one of the more interesting murder cases I was exposed to during my thirty-four-year police career.

The Joyce Lumas murder investigation consisted of some really good police work (combined with a bit of pure-D, unadulterated blind luck) that came about because of a bad gut feeling. Collectively, four experienced investigators felt the case just didn't smell right. They went the extra mile and then some, rather than just write the matter off as a missing person case. They knew it was not a case of a new wife who was simply fed up with her unemployed ex-con husband and just skying up. Had some other people been assigned this case it might not have gone as well as it did. The luck of the draw is a truism that exists in poker, rodeo rough stock riding, criminal investigation and prosecution. This information has been provided as some real food for thought and things to ponder upon.

Another point I would like to put out there is that the human animal is a predator. There are two types of animals in this world—predators and prey. Predators like wolves, bears, and big cats all have their eyes on the front of their heads. Prey animals like rabbits, deer, birds or mice have eyes on the sides of their heads. Look in the mirror. Which group do we human animals fall into? We in the western world want to hold ourselves out to be a civilized people. There are those among us, though, who never will make it to that level. My father told me that we Middle Americans are far too civilized for our own good. He said Americans think chickens are born without feathers, feet or heads and lie around in the grocery store on a piece of foam waiting for us to take them home and cook them. I have worked looking into the underbelly of the beast for thirty-five years. Being a street corner philosopher, I thought I might share these thoughts before we get down to the details of these specific murder cases.

Welcome to what was my world for many years. The cases re-surface from time to time, either when cold cases are cleared, or cases are re-tried following a conviction's reversal upon appeal. I now have a twenty-year-old murder that has finally cleared and will be going to trial soon. I guess homicide work is like being in the Mob—once in, never out. That and you will never see things in life as others do. You appreciate and understand your mortality better than most.

Since you are reading this book you obviously have an interest in crime, criminals and the investigation of both. The investigations into these career cases that follow are some of the most interesting stories I have come across in the thirty-four years I spent in law enforcement. Now sit back and have a good read.

•ROBERT LUMAS•

One hot, muggy night in Houston, Texas, uniformed HPD officers Scott "Doby" Dobyanski and Jimmy O'Brien were working the night shift out of the Beechnut Station. Their beat included a stretch of Westheimer Road that was known as "Sin Alley" by the area uniformed troops. Sin Alley was a stretch of road populated by several strip joints, a dirty book store or two with peep show video booths in the back, and a movie house that featured porn. This area was more or less a multi-service center for lower forms of life. The clientele in this area consisted of trashy women and degenerates of both genders.

Typically, wherever trashy women and degenerates hang out, you also find both drugs and drug dealers who associate with this lower class of people. Beyond that social circle, you get the predatory humans who are prone to rob dope dealers, club patrons and coin-operated machines that masquerade as women—the ones who often come away from a night's work carrying several hundred dollars in cash. Area uniformed cops made regular passes through the parking lots of those wonderful establishments, and on a pretty consistent basis came up with some good quality arrests. The concept here is that if you are looking to catch flies you need to hang around dung heaps.

On this particular night, Dobyanski and O'Brien sat at a traffic light at the corner of Hillcroft Avenue and Westheimer Road, waiting to turn west onto Westheimer. The stripped down police car they were riding in did not even have a radio in the dashboard. They made do with a portable, battery-operated "Good Time" radio that sat on top of the dash, held in place with rubber bands affixed to paper clips hooked into the windshield defroster/heater vents.

As they sat at the light they were looking directly toward a twenty-four-hour gas station across the intersection. A man at the walk-up pay window of the gas station turned and looked over his left shoulder. Next, he did a complete about face and sprinted approximately fifteen yards to a Chevrolet Camaro parked in the gas station lot. The uniformed cops watched as the man in question dove—Superman style—through the car's open passenger window. The driver of the Camaro sped off, spinning the tires as he pulled out onto Westheimer, in too much of a hurry to remember to turn on his headlights. Once on Westheimer—a busy, six-lane road—the driver slowed to a crawl and began to weave back and forth between different lanes of traffic. The cops pulled up behind the car and turned on their emergency lights. The Camaro continued westbound on Westheimer, but now at very slow rate of speed. A few blocks later, the driver began to weave back and forth across all six lanes of undivided traffic. Next, the slow moving muscle car jumped the far left curb and hit several cars parked in a strip club parking lot.

The officers pulled up behind the wrecked car, and carefully made their approach, each with a gun in one hand and a flashlight in the other. When they reached the car they discovered two men fighting in the back seat. The man they'd seen jump through the car's passenger window now had another man—sporting a serious gash on his forehead—in a headlock. The choker was calling out to the cops, "He tried to steal my car!" His victim, who was obviously losing the fight, immediately countered with, "I did not steal his car!"

Both men were handcuffed and questioned, and the officers determined the choker was, in fact, the registered owner of the car. It turned out that the loser of the fight had technically been telling the truth. He had not in actuality stolen the car. He'd just been unsuccessful in his attempt to steal it.

Scalp wounds bleed badly, so an ambulance was called for the auto thief, who had been identified as Robert Lumas. Upon examination, the ambulance crew advised the crook really needed several stitches to close the gash on his forehead. The suspect claimed he was a Marine Corps veteran and demanded to be taken to the Veteran's Administration Hospital for treatment.

Young officers Dobyanski and O'Brien were about to be introduced to a common scam used by crooks attempting to slip away from an arrest.

After Lumas was loaded up, the two officers followed the ambulance to the hospital. There they were advised that city, county and state police have no jurisdiction at Veteran's Administration hospitals, since they sit on federal reservations. Fortunately, most of the federal police at those locations are former cops and work well with local police agencies. Since VA cops have to call city cops from time to time to have drunks and problem children arrested, it benefits them to maintain good relationships with the locals. The VA police were asked to sit on Lumas while the city officers filed charges.

Once charges were filed, Sin Alley's unlucky auto thief

of the night became a ward of Harris County. A sheriff's deputy was dispatched to go pick him up. In the meantime, once Lumas got stitched up he was put into a holding cell at the VA hospital (yes, they have one there) until the deputy arrived. Lumas was later booked straight into the Harris County jail on an auto theft charge.

Once the two officers handed Lumas off to paramedics at the scene, that was the last they saw of him that night, which is the norm. Cops pick up the trash. The courts process it, and the prison system recycles it. Unless someone wants to go to trial and contest a charge, most cases like Lumas' are simply pled out for jail time or given probation. Uniformed officers often never know what happens to the cases they file.

Scott Dobyanski, a.k.a. Doby, went on to work in undercover on the Vice Squad night shift for a while and was later promoted to the rank of detective and assigned to the Homicide Division. While Dobyanski never saw Robert Lumas again on the night of the attempted auto theft, the two would eventually meet again. Lumas went on to pick up an assortment of criminal charges and even do prison time for the attempted murder of a man he would later claim had been his best friend in the world.

Such a friendship would be better passed on if at all possible.

A Missing Person Report

Houston resident Joyce Malone was reported missing by her eighteen-year-old daughter, Loretta King.

Any time an adult is reported missing, the Adult Missing Persons Unit makes sure that certain criteria are met before they formally issue an offense report and list the person in question as a bona fide missing person. Among the criteria are that the person must be missing for a certain number of days and the reporting party must have checked local hospitals as well as the city and county jails.

Loretta King had done all of that and made an offense report. While Loretta lived with her father and stepmother, she was very close to her mother and spoke with her daily. Loretta told police that although her mother was missing from her apartment, her car was still there. Further compounding Loretta's concern was the fact that her mother—who had never missed work—had not shown up to her place of employment, or even called in. The daughter suspected foul play and felt sure that her mother's dirt bag ex-convict boyfriend had something to do with her disappearance.

Missing adult cases can be tricky, because it is not illegal for an adult to go missing, and some adults who go missing do not want to be found. Once a report has been generated by a police agency the missing person is logged into state and national police databases as missing persons. Most of these cases resolve themselves in a day or two when the party in question reappears after a drunken or drug-related binge. The people in question may even go as far as to claim they were kidnapped and that they either escaped or were simply turned loose. When Joyce Malone did not surface after several days, the Missing Persons desk sent the case over to the Homicide Division. The evening shift lieutenant, Bobby Beck, assigned the case to two detectives named Scott "Doby" Dobyanski and Bobby "Cuz" Williams.

The 4 p.m. to midnight shift was comprised of mostly younger detectives, and seniority was generally a lot higher on the day shift. However, the evening shift made about fifty-eight percent of the yearly murder scenes in Houston, staffed with half the manpower of the day crew.

Doby and Cuz each had about three years in the Detective Bureau when this case was assigned to them. Doby was raised in rural Brazoria County near Alvin, Texas. Cuz Williams was raised in a rough part of north Houston. He went to Reagan High School where the male students were said to either go into police work or go on to wear white prison uniforms.

As with most cases of this sort, the investigation began by trying to locate witnesses over the phone. The detectives were unable to reach the reportee (daughter) so they moved on to calling the missing person's apartment in southwest Houston. They spoke to Robert Lumas, who advised he was in fact Joyce's husband, as they had been married a couple of weeks earlier. Lumas advised that he and the missing woman had been living together for a couple of years and recently decided to marry. He also told them he had attempted to report his new wife as missing but when he contacted police, he was advised a report had already been made.

Lumas detailed Joyce's disappearance by saying that on the previous Sunday morning he had gone to the store to get some breakfast and when he returned his wife was up and they visited for a bit. Then he left to go wash his car. When he returned, he noted Joyce's car was gone. After showering he answered a knock at the door and was greeted by his wife's best friend, Jackie Fry. Jackie told Lumas that she and Joyce had plans to go out, and she was there to pick up Joyce. Lumas said Joyce wasn't there, and that he did not know of his wife's whereabouts. Jackie told him she would wait outside for a little while and she left. Lumas told police that a few hours later he went outside and saw that Joyce's car was back in its parking space. He hadn't worried about her at that point, he said, figuring she'd returned and left with Jackie Fry.

Later that evening Jackie Fry called their apartment and asked for Joyce. She told Lumas that she'd never met up with her friend that day. Lumas told the detectives that the next morning he noticed two pieces of his luggage were missing and he found a couple of pawn shop tickets that indicated Joyce had pawned several pieces of jewelry. He added that Joyce's car keys were also missing.

Lumas went on to tell investigators that his wife was bi-sexual and had been involved with other women during the two years they had lived together, adding that their live-in arrangement prior to marriage had been an on again-off again situation. Then he dropped on the investigators that shortly after their marriage ceremony she had taken him to a lawyer where she signed her two cars over to him and signed a power of attorney giving him control over all her financial matters, including the two cars she registered in his name. Lumas said he did not understand her reasoning for doing this but he knew his wife had a bunch of outstanding bills. Before the interview concluded, Lumas gave investigators a list of names and phone numbers of friends of his wife. Among them was the name of a woman he claimed had a crush on his wife.

The next morning, the case was picked up by day shift detectives Larry Ott and David Collier. Ott and Collier were a couple of hard-working and experienced investigators whose personalities were sort of like opposite magnetic poles. Ott was somewhat retiring, and he was both a handyman and a weight lifter. In fact, Ott had built his own house from the ground up. Collier, on the other hand, was a tall, large, loud, bald-headed, beer-drinking, good-old-boy sort. He was also a CPA, and not the type to worry about his physique.

After picking up the case, the two detectives began

making phone calls and knocking on doors. Some of the names supplied by Robert Lumas were helpful but each person they contacted had rather limited information. Jackie Fry (Joyce's best friend) felt that something bad had happened to Joyce. She told the investigators Joyce adored her daughter Loretta, and would never have missed her daughter's high school graduation. Jackie went on to say Joyce had confided in her that Lumas had forbidden her to attend the upcoming graduation because Loretta had called him an "asshole." Jackie added that Joyce was afraid of Robert Lumas and that she (Jackie) had seen bruises where Lumas had abused Joyce in the past. On the day Joyce was reported to have disappeared, Jackie told detectives she had been sitting in the apartment complex parking lot waiting on Joyce to return—a detail that matched up with Lumas' version of events. While she was waiting for Joyce, she said she witnessed Lumas carrying a large plastic bag—filled with something obviously very heavy—out to his car. After placing the bag in the trunk of his car, Jackie said Lumas went back into the apartment, came out a short time later, this time with an overnight bag, got into the car and drove off. When the detectives asked Jackie if she knew about any jewelry Joyce owned, she said that Joyce never went anywhere without all of her jewelry, and when she was in her apartment she hid her valuables under a loose corner of the rug in the bathroom for safekeeping.

Collier and Ott were able to verify several details in Robert's story. The couple had indeed been married by a justice of the peace and they had met with an attorney. Detectives confirmed that Joyce had signed her cars over to Robert and signed a will leaving her earthly belongings to him. Lumas had answers for all questions asked of him, and nothing uncovered was really damning.

The evening shift detectives hit the pawn shop where Joyce had pawned her jewelry and the owner advised she was a regular at his place, frequently pawning her jewelry. On this most recent visit, Joyce told the pawnbroker she needed cash to get her poodle treated by a local veterinarian. After leaving the pawn shop, Dobyanski and Williams dropped by Joyce's apartment for an unannounced meeting with the less-than-grieving husband. When Lumas opened the door, bells went off in Doby's head. He knew the face, but did not know from where. It had been nine years since he'd arrested Lumas for auto theft. Back at the station, with a bit of research, Doby was able to find the auto theft case where he and Jimmy O'Brien filed on Lumas years earlier.

In phone conversations with detectives, Lumas mentioned a number of people who had been friends of his wife. The investigators found most of these people to be far from cooperative. Their reactions ran the gamut from slamming doors in the cops' faces to denying they even knew who the cops were talking about. This only clouded the situation. Those who did admit to knowing Joyce said she had friends who were openly gay and other friends who may have been closet cases. Others who knew Joyce reported that she did visit female bars on occasion.

The investigators noted in their reports—at various points—that nothing pointed to foul play, but that Robert Lumas was accused by several different people of changing his stories a bit, and generally not being trustworthy.

A check with Joyce Lumas' first husband, Chuck King (with whom their two daughters lived), indicated Joyce was very much heterosexual. He also told investigators that Joyce had a second husband named Malone, who moved back to France after their marriage ended. King also shared that their older daughter had, in fact, lived with Joyce until Robert Lumas made sexual advances toward her in the form of tearing off her clothes. Joyce's ex-husband, Chuck, and both of her daughters were very surprised Joyce had not told them about her marriage to Lumas.

Approximately two weeks after the investigation began, Lumas reported to the detectives that his missing wife had called collect to tell him she was now living in San Francisco, California and that she was never coming back. She told him not to try and find her, and that she was starting a new life. A check of phone records (via subpoena) indicated a collect call had been made to the couple's apartment on the date and time Lumas indicated. The call originated from a pay phone in Stockton, California. Lumas said that he was going on with his life, but since he was without a job he would have to move in with his parents. He was asked to take a polygraph exam, to which he agreed. He was immediately scheduled for one the next morning.

Lumas showed up on time the following morning, and the polygraph was performed. Upon completion, the examiner advised investigators that the results indicated deception on all questions regarding harm to Joyce Lumas, knowledge as to whether she had been killed, and if the respondent had anything to do with it. In order to keep Lumas from "lawyering up" or fleeing, Doby told Lumas he had passed the examination on all questions asked of him.

The case rocked along for a few weeks with no real leads—just a bad gut feeling that Joyce Lumas was dead and they simply could not prove it. At the time in Texas, you had to have a body to prove someone had been murdered, and the expression used in police and legal circles was "No body—no crime."

The first real break in this case came (as many often do) in the form of what is known in police circles as "The magic phone call." Many major cases get cleared from information that originates from a phone call. People who commit crimes often brag to friends, wives or girlfriends. Then the guilty party may mess over said friend, wife or girlfriend. Sometimes people get religion, or just can't abide killers or people harming innocent others. For whatever reason, many big breaks come from someone "dropping a dime" on the guilty party. In the Lumas case, the "magic phone call" came by way of a phone message from a detective named Jim Castles in Stockton, California. This was the first real break in a case that would have more twists and turns than a mountain road.

Doby and Williams contacted Castles, who told them he had an informant with whom a recent Houston resident was now living. That former Houston resident was a white female named Mary Ellen Kroft, who was a half-sister of the informant. The informant also shared that Mary was the current girlfriend of Robert Lumas, and was known to have recently called Lumas from a pay phone in Stockton, pretending to be Joyce Lumas.

The juicy details didn't end there. Detective Castles also learned from the informant that Lumas (the less-than-grieving husband) had been calling Mary at the house where she had been staying, discussing the police investigation with her. The informant said she'd overheard Lumas and Mary talking about disposing of a body. All this information was reportedly coming by way of the informant and her husband as they'd overheard portions of conversations between Lumas and their house guest.

Police records division checks showed Mary Kroft to have been a sexual assault complainant two years earlier, at which time Robert Lumas was her boyfriend. After clearing with their supervisor, the detectives made reservations to fly to California a couple of days later. In the meantime, they had several discussions with Chuck Rosenthal, the chief prosecutor of the Special Crimes section of the Harris County District Attorney's Office, about how to proceed. They also obtained a grand jury subpoena for Mary Kroft to testify as to her knowledge in this matter and another subpoena for the telephone records of Lumas' apartment phone. Jim Castles provided numbers for four pay phones from which Kroft allegedly placed the collect call while pretending to be Joyce Lumas. One of those numbers appeared on phone company records as being the collect call number from Stockton, California. Murder investigations are subject to long-term review, so good police work is critical. You don't want to retry a case every five or ten years just because some procedure was not followed to the letter. For that reason, a good investigator checks and re-checks with prosecutors rather than figuring he knows it all and screwing something up permanently. Those who don't check and re-check will screw up major cases from time to time.

After flying to California on a low-budget airline (that should have been in some third world country), Doby and Williams rented a car and met with Jim Castles of Stockton PD. He brought the Houston cops up to speed as to what his informant had relayed to him. Mary Kroft was in his town, with no car, was unemployed, flat broke and living with a relative. Reportedly, Kroft just showed up on her relative's front porch unannounced, with a suitcase in her hand. Castles first set up a meeting with the informant, who was not only a relative of Kroft's, but also a down-the-street neighbor of Castles.

California Pay Dirt (Sort of)

Jim Castles could not have been more helpful. He first arranged a meeting between the Houston investigators and his informant, Mary Kroft's relative. Castles was tied up on another case, so a Detective Wingo of the Stockton PD was assigned to give the Houston cops a hand. According to the informant, Mary had been getting regular phone calls from Robert Lumas in Houston. Both the informant and her husband had overhead portions of Mary's phone conversations that sounded very suspicious. Overhearing phrases like, "What have the police said?" as well as discussions about "Do they suspect anything?" and "Have they found the body?" made the informant and her husband more than just a little uncomfortable.

Accompanied by the Stockton detective, Doby and Cuz went to the informant's house and asked to speak with Mary. Wingo told her they needed to speak with her about a matter that occurred in Houston. She agreed to talk with them but asked what they wanted to talk with her about, and Wingo replied that it would be best if she accompanied them to the police station. She agreed and rode with them to the Stockton Central Police station.

At the station, Williams and Dobyanski advised Mary that they wanted to question her regarding any information she had about Joyce Lumas, Joyce's disappearance, Robert Lumas, and any role he may have played in Joyce's disappearance. Mary agreed to speak with the investigators, and a court reporter from a California superior court was brought in. In California, using a court reporter was (and still is) the standard procedure when taking statements. Since laws regarding admissibility of statements—in oral or written forms—vary from state to state, Williams and Dobyanski wanted to cover all their bases. Therefore, when Mary's rights were read to her, the Texas cops included the wording "You have the right to end this interview at any time." Although Mary's statement was taken in California, where that verbiage is not required, any statement taken without that right included would be completely worthless for criminal prosecution back in Texas.

In summary, Mary's statement was that she had been Robert Lumas' girlfriend for a couple of years and that he had been talking about "disposing of" his wife. In their conversations, Robert told Kroft that he wanted to kill Joyce, and he shared where and how he'd thought of disposing of her body. Mary also she said their conversations had included discussions of both wills and powers of attorney.

Mary stated that Lumas got her a plane ticket to California and directed her to stay with a relative of hers. A couple of days after arriving in Stockton, Robert called and directed her to place a collect call to his apartment from a pay phone. She was to say that she was Joyce and that she was all right, but that she was never coming back to Texas. After Mary placed the call, just like he'd asked her, Lumas called her there in California and told her she did not have to worry about Joyce any longer. Mary obviously did not like talking about Joyce. The Texas detectives speculated this was because Kroft was "the other woman." One of the most interesting things Mary related to the Houston investigators during that interview was that the reason Lumas had her travel to California—specifically to call him collect—was that he felt investigators had probably tapped his home phone line and Mary's call would give him the out he needed and bolster his claim of innocence.

Mary stated that Robert called her several times from Houston while she was staying with her relatives, but only once did she call his apartment, and when she got his message recorder she hung up. Lumas called her that same evening and she mentioned she'd called his apartment, but had not left a message. She said Lumas went completely ballistic and told her she had just sent the both of them to prison, then he hung up on her. Mary related that during some of their conversations, Lumas asked her that if he went through with "this" would she be able to handle questioning by the police. She reportedly answered that she wanted to be left out of "it" and that yes, she could handle what may take place and talking with the police.

After her statement, Kroft was asked if she wanted to return to Houston the next morning with Williams and Dobyanski. She said she did, and the Houston cops arranged for her to have a seat on their return flight. She was told by the Houston cops that when she spoke with Robert next, to tell him her relative in California had asked her to leave because their home was just too small for an uninvited guest. If Lumas were to ask where the money for her plane fare had come from, she was to tell him she had begged it from her sister Donna (with whom she would be living, in Jacinto City, Texas).

Meanwhile Back Home in Sodom

Before leaving California, the Houston detectives called Homicide and arranged for Detective Larry Ott to pick them up at Houston's Hobby airport. Upon landing, Ott picked them up and drove them to 201 Fannin Street, where they met with Special Crimes Prosecutor Chuck Rosenthal. From there, Mary was taken to her sister's house in Jacinto City, Texas, a short distance east of Houston.

A polygraph exam was set up for ten o'clock the next morning for Mary Kroft. After two hours, the polygraph examiner told investigators that prior to starting the exam, Mary volunteered that Lumas had given her two pieces of Joyce Lumas' jewelry before she left for Stockton. Results of the polygraph indicated she was truthful regarding having no knowledge of the missing person's whereabouts, and not taking part in "disposing" of Joyce Lumas. Chuck Rosenthal was advised of the test results and he immediately suggested investigators take Mary to Galveston, where she had told detectives that she and Lumas had gone crabbing and fishing in the past. At that time, she had also commented that "he took all his girlfriends crabbing in Galveston." Rosenthal's reasoning for the trip to Galveston is that suspects will often go to an area they are comfortable with to dump bodies—at least for their first kills. When you work on a serial killer, his first body will often be dumped in an area he knows pretty well, and the bodies thereafter tend to be dumped farther away from his comfort zone or killing ground.

Ott, Doby, and Williams loaded up in a city car and headed to Galveston Island, with Mary in tow. Mary told them Lumas' favorite place to go crabbing was on Pelican Island, and that it was a long distance from the highway. None of the cops even knew where Pelican Island was, so they touched base with the Galveston County Sheriff's Department's Organized Crime Unit. Organized Crime and Narcotics units are always helpful because they chase crooks into multiple jurisdictions. They also get involved in shooting situations more often than others because of the class of criminal they deal with. As a detective, it is a good thing to be on friendly terms with folks that are going to investigate your shootings and present your cases to grand juries.

The Galveston County troops met up with the Houston detectives and their witness, and led them out to the area in question. Mary pointed the way from Broadway Street, the main drag of Galveston Island, to a short causeway leading onto the barrier island. They drove from Pelican Road to

Bradner Road, and then onto a dirt road that came to a dead end at a large illegal dump site. From the illegal dump site, there was an intersection of three roads leading away from the refuse area. Mary pointed to a road leading off to the northwest. After approximately half a mile, the hard surface turned to deep, dry sand that was difficult to drive on.

They drove another four to five miles to a major bend in the road, where Mary told them to stop. This, she said, was where Robert liked to fish and crab. The area consisted of many hundreds of acres of open fields, grassy marsh fields and barren sand. The shoreline was also close by. They all got out of their cars and walked about for a short while, quickly realizing that a search of the area would take multiple people and several days, at the very least. There are no inhabitants on that portion of Pelican Island, and the nearest permanent structure is a Coast Guard station several miles away as the crow flies. Detectives realized they had a better chance of buying a winning lottery ticket than finding witnesses to any burial—if one had even occurred. A helicopter search would be their best shot.

The detectives took Mary Kroft back to her sister's house and contacted Chuck Rosenthal for guidance. He suggested she record all of her telephone calls with Lumas in order to see if he might admit to anything relating to where he disposed of the body.

During this time in Texas' legal history, if police directed someone to talk with a possible suspect and record their conversations, those conversations were admissible in a court of law as an admission on the part of the defendant. Not long after, a Supreme Court ruling voided this practice. It noted that if people were acting as agents for the police and recording conversations with a possible suspect, the suspect would have to be advised of his Miranda rights prior to that conversation, if the recording was to be placed into evidence. However, it is legal in Texas, as well as most states, to tape record a telephone conversation if at least one party to that conversation has knowledge a recording is being made. In other states, recording a conversation without someone's knowledge constitutes wiretapping.

Lumas was now living with his parents and unemployed. Dobyanski and Williams hooked a recorder up to the phone in Mary's sister's home and showed Mary how to use it. The two investigators stopped by the Lumas family home in southwest Houston that afternoon to kick-start conversations about the investigation. They were met at the door by Robert's family and were advised he was not home. When they advised the family (mother, father and sister) they were looking into Joyce Lumas' disappearance and treating it as a possible homicide, Robert's sister (who was reportedly nothing short of stunningly beautiful) blurted out, "If that son-of-a-bitch messes up my wedding memories I'll never forgive him." The detectives asked her how he would do such a thing, and she explained that Robert was scheduled to be the wedding singer at her upcoming nuptials. The detectives asked that the family have Robert call them when he got time. They figured applying some pressure might spark some interesting telephone conversations between Lumas and Kroft.

When Doby and Williams got back to their office they called Mary (putting her on the speaker phone) and asked about Lumas being a wedding singer. Mary told them he had a wonderful singing voice and was both a wedding singer and an Elvis impersonator. After hanging up with Kroft, Bobby Williams broke out in a pretty good rendition of Elvis' hit song, "Love Me Tender." Dobyanski was not terribly impressed and said that he thought "You Ain't

Nothin' But a Hound Dog" would be more fitting regarding the Robert Lumas he knew and loathed.

Lumas called Homicide almost immediately after detectives got off the phone with Mary Kroft. He wanted to know if there were any breaks in the case and he was advised there were not. Lumas said Loretta King had been slandering him by saying that he'd had something to do with her mother's disappearance and insinuating he'd killed Joyce. Detectives told him not worry about it. Lumas went on to say that he was trying to get an annulment, and that he had heard there was a grace period of thirty days following a marriage. He also said that period had run out for him and he was trying to figure out something. Lumas closed the conversation by saying he was trying to pay off some bills he acquired in his short marriage to Joyce and then move on with his life. The cops said they would contact him as soon as they had any news in the case, and asked him to call when, or if, he similarly received any new information.

In the days that followed, Lumas called Mary ad nauseum, telling her he loved her and wanted to meet with her and hold her close. He repeatedly asked to come to her sister's home to visit. Detectives saw this as an opportunity, so they arranged for the Special Crimes Unit to wire the front room of her sister's place so conversations could be monitored from outside the building. When Robert came to visit, the monitored conversations consisted of Robert talking with his darling about his job prospects, and also about wanting to have sex with Mary. On one particular night, the two left the apartment to go to a restaurant down the road and afterward, Lumas brought Mary back home, and he left. The front room recorder was removed but the phone recorder stayed.

The phone recorder yielded some interesting revelations. Lumas bragged that he had access to the police offense reports through his brother Mike, who worked at the central police station. He claimed the cops had nothing. He went on to say that there was "no body" and "no evidence of foul play." Lumas also threatened that if things got bad he would just put the whole thing off on Mary. Mister Wonderful spoke about somebody he called "the little midget" who he also called by the name Aaron. Lumas claimed he had been polygraph tested by the cops already and had passed. He went on to tell Mary that if she were asked to take one, he wanted to "prep" her beforehand. He told Mary that Aaron knew what to say if questioned or polygraphed, and would not talk. The hostile tone Lumas used when talking to Mary had both Doby and Williams concerned. They were beginning to fear for the safety of their only possible witness in this case.

Doby and Williams met with Mary and determined that Robert's brother Manuel (Mike) Lumas did, in fact, work at the police station, as some sort of civilian employee. The "little midget," also known as Aaron, was determined (by asking Mary) to be Aaron "Jack" McFarland, a longtime friend of Lumas who worked as a new car salesman. The two friends had been estranged for over a year but had recently buried the hatchet. They had been at odds over the theft of money from Aaron's girlfriend's purse, and someone trying to scam Aaron's mother's credit card information. Aaron suspected Lumas in both events and made no bones about telling him so.

Because Lumas was acting hostile towards Mary, the only witness yet discovered in their case, Doby and Cuz Williams contacted the district attorney's office with their concerns. DA Rosenthal and Terry Wilson kicked the topic around, and finally suggested moving Mary Kroft out of town. In fact, the Harris County DA's office even footed the bill for Mary to stay in a motel called The Huntsville Inn, located about seventy-five miles north of Houston, in Huntsville, Texas.

A couple of days after booking Mary Kroft into the Huntsville Inn under an assumed name, Doby and Williams interviewed Manuel "Mike" Lumas at the central police station. The missing person report status was checked, and investigators confirmed it had been coded confidential early on in the investigation, which meant no one other than authorized personnel had reviewed it. Mike Lumas had no access to their police report. Furthermore, he was quite cooperative. When asked if he knew a woman named Mary or Mo, he said he did, and that she was a girlfriend of his brother. Mike went on to say that it was his understanding she was cooperating with the district attorney's office and was staying in Huntsville. Then he dropped another bombshell on them, saying he had been told all this by his brother Robert, who was talking with Mary on a regular basis.

The next day Doby, Williams and Larry Ott drove to Huntsville and checked Mary out of the motel. Motel phone records showed Mary had made two calls to her sister in Jacinto City and seven to Houston PD Homicide. The motel clerk advised them that if Mary had made a collect call that it would not have shown up on the motel's call register. Upon their return to Houston, the detectives drove directly to the Special Crimes Section of the DA's office. They reviewed the case at hand with Wilson and Rosenthal and determined a course of action. The decision was made to subpoena Mary, Manuel Lumas and Aaron "Jack" McFarland to appear before a grand jury. This step would lock each into their testimony, and they would be subject to felony charges if their testimony was found to be untrue.

Robert's Best Friend

Aaron "Jack" McFarland was served with a grand jury subpoena at the car dealership where he worked off Houston's Northwest Freeway. He accepted the subpoena and agreed to accompany detectives to the Special Crimes Section of the District Attorney's Office. Aaron discussed the case (seemingly openly) with the prosecutors. He was then transported to the polygraph examiner's office at the Houston Police Department. The cops lucked out and found an examiner who had just had a cancellation. After completing the polygraph, the examiner's conclusion was that McFarland showed some signs of deception on the following questions:

Do you know where Joyce is?
Did you hurt Joyce?
Did you see Joyce last month?
Did you cause Joyce's disappearance?
Did you hurt Joyce last month?

McFarland was advised that he showed deception on those questions and he could not explain the examiner's findings. He contended he had been telling the truth throughout the whole of the interview. Next, McFarland voluntarily gave a tape recorded statement to the investigators. In it, he said that he and Robert Lumas had been friends all of their lives, growing up in southwest Houston. He considered Lumas his best friend, and he also knew Robert's girlfriend Mary Kroft. McFarland said that Robert told him that his wife Joyce had just taken off without any warning. She then was supposed to have called a week or so later and told Robert that she was in San Francisco and was not coming back.

McFarland said that he felt Robert may well have done something bad to Joyce, but that Robert had never come right out and told him that. He said that some statements made by Lumas contradicted one another. Robert also told him that Mary had flown out to California and called him in Houston, while pretending to be Joyce. McFarland further said he had been told by Robert that Joyce was not coming back, and noted that Robert kept mentioning Galveston. However, McFarland added, Robert would not elaborate about Joyce not coming back or specifics about Galveston. McFarland said when he asked Robert questions as to whether he was involved in harming or killing Joyce, that Robert would only answer, "Aaron, I don't want to involve you."

McFarland went on to say Robert told him that Mary had called him from Huntsville and told him she was cooperating with the district attorney's office, which had relocated her to the Huntsville Inn. Lumas also informed McFarland he was leaving town and headed for Seattle, Washington.

The investigators then took McFarland back to the DA's office where prosecutors Wilson and Rosenthal reviewed the taped interview. They told McFarland his statement was somewhat inconsistent regarding everything he had told them before. They wanted him to return to their offices in six days and be prepared to discuss the matter at length. McFarland agreed and returned to work.

Six days later, as promised, McFarland came into the DA's office, and the investigators picked up Mary and brought her in, as directed by Rosenthal. She was brought into the Special Crimes Section and seated in the office with McFarland, and Assistant District Attorneys Wilson and Rosenthal. McFarland advised Mary (in front of the assistant district attorneys) that he was telling everything to the authorities and holding nothing back. He told her that she needed to do the same. He advised her that Robert had gone into detail with him about her calling him from a pay phone in Huntsville, and how the district attorney's office was keeping her at the Huntsville Inn. He added that Lumas had told him she was working with the DA and the police, and that Robert told him that he was leaving town and heading to Seattle, Washington.

Mary Kroft was asked to explain what McFarland had just told them. Mary admitted calling Robert Lumas from a pay phone at a restaurant next door to the motel. She first called her sister, who determined where Robert was, so that she could reach him. Mary said Robert knew everything about the investigation already. She said Robert "manipulated" her into telling him everything she had done and what she had said to the authorities. She admitted that he told her he was going to Seattle and would be staying with a friend named Will.

Rosenthal directed Mary to have a seat in the outside lobby waiting room. Assistant District Attorneys Rosenthal and Wilson discussed the matter and decided their best course of action was to file felony charges of credit card abuse against Mary Kroft for her involvement in the use of Joyce Sloan Lumas' credit card to fly to California. There is nothing like a bit of leverage to get the attention and cooperation of a reluctant witness.

Rosenthal typed up the charges there in his office, and they were sworn to by Doby. Mary Kroft was transported to the Homicide Division at the Central Station and advised of the charges being filed against her. She was allowed to call her lawyer and was placed in the city jail. Doby was a bit astounded by it all. That evening at home, he discussed the recent developments in the case with his wife. He told her he just could not understand how Mary Kroft could act the way she had. His wife looked at him and flatly said, "You just don't get it. She's in love with him—and if she's sleeping with him she's telling him everything she's doing."

The next day, Doby and Williams went to the Fiscal Affairs office at the main police station and met with Manuel "Mike" Lumas. They told Mike they had information that his brother Robert had left town and was possibly headed to Seattle, Washington. They also told him that they had heard his parents had supposedly given Robert money so that he could leave town. Mike Lumas said he knew nothing of Robert leaving or getting money from his parents. He did volunteer that he knew of someone named Will that Robert had been in the military with, but that he thought Will had recently moved to South America.

Mike Lumas told the investigators that just minutes before they'd walked in, his mother had called him saying that the news had just reported that Robert was now a suspect in his wife's disappearance. Mike said he would immediately call his parents individually and see if he could get more information as to Robert's whereabouts, and whether his folks had given Robert money. The two detectives told the brother they would be down in Homicide and asked that he call them as soon as he touched base with his folks. Within an hour, Mike Lumas called, saying his mother admitted giving Robert all the cash she had on hand, which consisted of one hundred and thirty dollars, but she claimed not to know where he was. A meeting was set up with the Lumas family to meet at their home the next evening. Mike Lumas set the meeting time late enough so that he too could be present.

The media is allowed the use of an office located at the central police station. Eric Hansen, a reporter for the Houston Chronicle, had been closely following the Joyce

Lumas case, and regularly asked the assigned investigators about it. It was Hansen who put out that Robert was being considered a suspect, and subsequently the local TV stations picked up on it. All media stations look forward to "scooping" their competitors, and they all check their competition's releases and lead stories for something their own people might have missed.

Galveston Pay Dirt

Collier, Ott, Dobyanski and Williams decided they needed to make a real attempt at searching the Pelican Island area that both Aaron and Mary had talked about. They had been working on the Joyce Lumas case whenever they could, but all four were still getting assigned new murder cases on a regular—sometimes weekly—basis. The investigators' days off rotated monthly, and when the time came that all four had the same weekend off, they decided to make a Saturday day trip to search for the remains of their missing person. To a man, they knew she was dead.

Ott and Collier were regular partners, as were Williams and Dobyanski. The four traveled to the island in two city cars and met just over the Pelican Island Causeway. The barrier island consisted of several thousand acres, which meant that to conduct a thorough search, the area would need to be divided into a grid and searched one section at a time, using a large group of searchers for each section.

The men started at the illegal dump site—a pretty good ways into the island—with one pair each at either end of the trash berm and working their way toward the center. Unfortunately, this initial sweep yielded no worthwhile discoveries. It was warm day, so Collier and Ott had brought along an ice chest full of Budweiser beer to ward off the possible effects of dehydration. After their sweep of the dump area the men moved down a side dirt road. This portion of the search was not really well organized.

As they searched, Doby kept being drawn to an area away from their main search area, so Doby broke away from the group to follow his hunch. A short ways down the road, Doby spotted a drainage ditch that intersected the road they were on. The ditch was six to eight feet deep and ran under the roadbed by way of a forty-two-inch concrete culvert. The ditch was dry, so Doby made his way down to get a closer look. As he got near the bottom, he saw there had obviously been a substantial fire inside the edge of the concrete culvert. In fact, the upper edge of the culvert was highly charred from flames and smoke. On top of the fire site was a large piece of tin with some metal coils, similar to those on the back of a refrigerator, sitting atop it. Doby flipped the piece of tin over with a stick and saw under it what appeared to be some possible burned stands of hair and fragments of bones—bones that looked big enough to be human.

Excited, Doby called out to his fellow investigators. Collier, Ott and Williams gathered around, and after an initial inspection, agreed he'd likely found what appeared to be human remains. Now they just needed to determine if that someone was Joyce Lumas, or some other poor soul.

Ott rubbed his jaw, pondered the situation for a moment, then turned to Williams and said, "Cuz, we heard about the Elvis routine you did up in Homicide a while back. If this really turns out to be Joyce Lumas I wanna hear you sing "I got a hunka hunka burning love." Homicide detectives' humor is a rough defense mechanism that is really difficult for outsiders to grasp, and gallows humor is about as good a description of it that you can find.

Collier called Houston Homicide and they in turn contacted the Galveston Police Department asking for assistance. Doby would later confide to the other detectives that he felt as if he had been drawn, or led, to that charred concrete culvert. He said he had no idea if it was divine guidance or cop's intuition, but something kept pulling him to the area they had not really planned to search.

Once the discovery was called in, Galveston's city and county authorities responded in spades. Showing up at the possible murder scene was an assistant district attorney, a medical examiner's investigator, a crime scene unit, an arson investigator, one patrolman and a uniformed sergeant. The arson investigator got an immediate positive reading of hydrocarbon (indicating gasoline) and flammable materials. The medical examiner's investigator and one of the uniformed officers gathered the obvious remains and placed them in a body bag. There were also ten sterile one-gallon paint cans filled with sand and debris found in and around the site of the skeletal fragments. Then twelve plastic bags were shoveled up from the inside of the culvert for crime lab examination as to additional evidence. These bags, when examined later, contained various bits of evidence, including possible human teeth, a scrap of burned cloth with an attached zipper, a fishing weight, and a spark plug. As the crime scene unit collected evidence, at least three local Houston news helicopters hovered overhead.

After clearing the scene the detectives retired to an establishment along the Galveston Seawall that specialized in adult beverages. The Houston cops enjoyed a quiet, peaceful celebration until the six o'clock news appeared on the large-screen TV hanging over the bar. Breaking news was the discovery of possible charred human remains on Pelican Island. One of the other club patrons looked at the TV, where a reporter was interviewing Collier, then turned toward the investigators and called out, "Hey, those guys right there are the ones on TV." There was no doubt it was big, bald-headed Dave Collier, with his booming rough voice and all. At this point, the Homicide troops felt it best to leave before the questions from other bar patrons began.

More Gifts from God (or Just Blind Luck)

Later that evening, the nightly news on all three major Houston stations featured the story of charred bones having been found on Pelican Island during a search conducted by Houston Homicide. Following the news coverage, investigators received a couple of exceptional breaks in the case.

A Pasadena, Texas resident called the Homicide front desk and spoke to Detective Ken Johnson. The man told Johnson he and a friend had been wade fishing on Pelican Island ten days before the charred bones were found and had come across a five-gallon plastic bucket containing part of a human skull. He said the skull had no lower jaw attached to it and all of the teeth were missing from the upper jaw. He added that a helicopter was circling overhead, which made them nervous, so they left the skull on a pinnacle of sand where the beach had eroded, but kept the bucket.

The skull had been discovered again a few days later by a man walking the beach with his dog. He found it in the sand, partially buried, and turned it over to the Galveston police, who took it to the Galveston County Medical Examiner's Office. The skull in question would wait there for the Houston Homicide guys who met with the chief medical examiner, Dr. Korndorfer, two days after the cremation site was discovered.

The same night the fisherman called Homicide, a second call came in, this time from a Galveston police officer named Riedel. He advised Detective Johnson that a couple of months before, he, his brother, and another off-duty officer had gone to Pelican Island to do some target shooting. They had been driving down a dirt road and rolled up on a guy standing by a culvert where a smoky fire was burning. Riedel said they stopped and asked the man in question what he was doing. The man (whose description closely matched Robert Lumas) said someone had built a fire and he was just checking it out. Riedel said that the guy seemed nervous and spoke in what Riedel called a "goofy sounding" foreign accent that struck Riedel as fake. The man's nervous demeanor was pronounced enough that the off-duty cop wrote down the license number of the car parked near the fire. That license number came back registered to Joyce Lumas' Lincoln Continental.

After learning of these new developments, Ott, Dobyanski, and Williams loaded up and headed to Galveston to review the findings of the medical examiner. Collier, in the meantime, drove to Texas City—also in Galveston County, approximately ten miles north of Galveston—to meet with the two off-duty officers and the civilian who had driven up on the mystery man tending a fire. Dr. Korndorfer, the Galveston County medical examiner, had examined the remains and declared them to be human, but had not yet found anything that would yield a positive identification.

Korndorfer was sifting through the cans collected at the recovery site by using a spaghetti colander to separate sand from possible evidence. When the buckets were collected, the Galveston arson investigators told the Houston troops to hold one can back so they could test it for the actual fuel used to burn the body. The Homicide guys, however, forgot to tell this to Dr. Korndorfer. The medical examiner told the Houston guys to go grab lunch because he had at least an hour to go through the stuff he'd already found. When they returned he was pouring the last can (the one they were saving for Arson) through the colander and mixing it with all the other sand.

As he sifted the last can, Korndorfer hit the jackpot. He found three complete teeth, two porcelain tooth caps, and a tooth root—evidence that gave him the best chance of making a positive identification. Had detectives saved the can for the Arson lab, they may have lost their only real evidence. Again, it was as if some sort of luck or outside force had prevailed. Upon finding the dental remnants, Korndorfer's actual comment was, "We got him."

After the medical examiner collected what he needed, Ott took custody of the dental evidence.

Dr. Korndorfer reported that the skull found on the beach not far from the charred bones was indeed that of a white female, and close in age to Joyce Lumas. He also confirmed that the skull had been charred in a fire. However, the skull could not be positively identified as the skull of Joyce Lumas, since DNA is destroyed when a body is cremated, leaving only calcified bone.

While Ott, Doby, and Williams were meeting with Dr. Korndorfer, Collier was in Texas City preparing a photo array to present to his witnesses. The array was comprised of six mug shots–Robert Lumas and five other men who closely resembled him. Officer Riedel and his brother each identified Robert Lumas as the man with the false-sounding foreign accent that they had seen by the fire. The other off-duty officer could only say Lumas looked like the man in question but he could not be positive. His identification, therefore, was noted to be tentative.

Investigators could now put Lumas at the cremation site. Ott drove from Galveston to Houston and directly to the office of Dr. Frank Carpos, Joyce Lumas' dentist. Dr. Carpos looked at the evidence and confirmed the pieces could be tied to dental work he had done on Joyce Lumas.

Things were coming together in a hurry. What's more, Mary Kroft was due to testify before the Grand Jury of the 262nd District Court the very next day.

The Whole Truth and Nothing But the Truth (If They Are Forced To)

The night before Mary Kroft was scheduled to testify before the grand jury, Doby received a call from Mary's sister, Donna Martin. Donna was privy to some very damning information in this case that had not yet come out—information she knew Mary would not volunteer if she were not pressured into doing so. In fact, Donna Martin's actual words were, "My sister is nothing but Jacinto City white trash, and there's nothing lower than white trash. She was raised better, but she wants to live and act like she does. If you don't have her by the short hairs, she's not gonna tell you everything, just enough to get you off her case."

Donna related that the evening before Mary flew to California, the two women had gone out on the town together first to dinner, and then to a night club. At one point in the evening, Mary told Donna that something had happened, and that Robert was going to kill his wife Joyce. His plan, Mary said, was to drug her and then burn her body in a garbage can. At the end of the evening, Mary asked Donna to drive her to Robert's apartment, and being the doting older sister, she reluctantly agreed. They went to his apartment and knocked, but no one answered the door. The two women noted that Robert's Oldsmobile was gone from its parking place, so they assumed he was gone, and they left.

Donna took Mary to her apartment, where she stayed overnight. The next morning Mary called Robert at his apartment and the two arranged a meeting. Donna then drove Mary to a convenience store where Mary met with Robert in the parking lot for about thirty minutes. When Mary got back in Donna's car, Mary told her sister that she was going to California but had no money. Donna gave her twenty-five dollars and then drove her to the parking lot of Robert's apartment complex where she dropped her off (suitcase in hand).

Immediately after collecting Donna Martin's statement, investigators contacted District Attorney Chuck Rosenthal at home. Rosenthal was to prosecution what zealots are to religion. He took calls at home from detectives and narcotics officers all hours of the day and night. His rule, however, was that any call made to him at home had better be damned important, and not something the district attorney on duty at the 24-hour intake section could not take care of. On this particular night, Rosenthal gladly took the call, and in turn contacted Mary Kroft's attorney to discuss Mary's upcoming appearance in front of the grand jury. In Texas, knowingly lying to a grand jury constitutes the felony crime of aggravated perjury. Furthermore, the way the law is written, a conviction of aggravated perjury comes with no possibility of probation.

The following morning, Mary Kroft was sworn in as a witness before a grand jury investigating the death of Joyce Lumas. Mary told the grand jury basically the same story she had told police, including the same information her sister Donna had given Dobyanski. Following that, Mary dropped a bombshell. She testified that Robert Lumas confided in her that he had strangled his wife Joyce while inside their apartment. After she was dead, he wrapped her body in several large plastic lawn or leaf bags. The following morning, Lumas carried Joyce's body out to his Oldsmobile and put her in the trunk. Mary's testimony was consistent with the eyewitness account of Jackie Fry, who reported seeing Lumas carry a heavy bag to his car trunk the morning she was to meet Joyce to go shopping.

Mary added that Lumas told her he drove to Galveston where he soaked Joyce's body in gasoline and burned it. He returned to Galveston on the following two Sundays where he burned the remains again on each trip. Mary further testified that Robert told her he was going to Seattle to live with a friend named Will, and as soon as he could, he would send her a plane ticket so she could join him. A few grand jury members posed questions to Mary, then she was allowed to leave.

Rosenthal drew up a warrant for the arrest of Robert Lumas, which was sworn to and signed by detective Dobyanski. Doby delivered the warrant to Judge Ted Poe who signed the warrant, making it valid. The intake section of the Harris County District Attorney's office assigned the case a docket number and set the bond at one hundred thousand dollars. Robert Lumas was now officially wanted and charged.

However, in spite of the warrant and official charges, their suspect was also now missing in action. The next day, Doby and Williams contacted the suspect's brother, Mike Lumas, who set up a meeting with the rest of his family. The meeting was scheduled for 8:30 p.m. the following day.

Aaron McFarland came into the Homicide office at 4:00 p.m. the next afternoon and gave a sworn statement. Aaron said that even when he asked Robert Lumas point blank if he had killed his wife, Lumas never actually confessed to killing Joyce Lumas. Robert's only response to McFarland's's question was, "I don't want to get you involved Aaron." However, McFarland added, Robert did tell him that he had burned a body (never saying *whose* body) down on Galveston Island. Robert further confided in McFarland that while he was in the process of burning this body down on the island, a truck with two or three men in it drove up and asked what he was doing. Robert reportedly adopted a thick Mexican accent while talking to the men in the truck, attempting to disguise himself. McFarland told investigators that he'd gotten really freaked out by Lumas when he asked questions like, "Aaron have you ever seen a body burn? It just sizzles and goes *pssssst*" and "Aaron, have you ever seen the inside of a skull?"

Since the conversations between Aaron McFarland and Lumas were private—not hearsay—all conversations included in Aaron McFarland's statement would be admissible in court.

The meeting with the Lumas family later that day was not productive. The head of the household, Manuel Lumas Sr., said he had just returned from Mexico City where he had been looking for Robert. He had heard that Robert had been there during the last week visiting relatives named Eloy and Mario Chavez. The Chavez brothers said Robert had in fact been there, but had left and they had no idea where he'd gone. Mrs. Lumas said that Robert got a phone call late one night from Mary Kroft. Robert confided in her that Mary had gotten him into some trouble involving credit card fraud and that he was leaving town.

Their suspect had given his mother power of attorney over his cars and personal affairs. She said she had given him all the cash she had on hand (which amounted to $140) and he left. As Robert had given his mother power of attorney over the cars, the investigators got his mom to sign 'consent to search' forms for both vehicles. Consequently, Lumas' Oldsmobile and Joyce's Lincoln were towed to the HPD print stall for processing.

With the suspect wanted and charged with murder he was listed nationally as wanted (under his given name as well as any aliases he'd used in the past), and was charged by the FBI with Unlawful Flight to Avoid Prosecution. If Lumas had fled the state—or country—extradition was not going to be a problem.

During their investigation, the four investigators hit every possible angle they could think of or dream up. They spoke to any and all friends they could identify, bondsmen, and old girlfriends. One former girlfriend with whom Robert had lived for a time described Robert as a "manipulator" who had a way of working people. She said he got people to do things for him "to prove they loved him."

Following up on Mary Kroft's testimony, investigators sought out Will from Seattle and determined he had been working in Alaska and would not be returning to the Lower 48 for at least another month or so. Will from Seattle actually turned out to be a smoke screen, intended to send the cops in the wrong direction. The detectives cataloged all the evidence and laid out the case for prosecution, because they felt certain when they caught Robert Lumas, he would be ready to put on a show during his trial. It was in fact determined that eight days before Lumas was filed on, Robert and his father had gone to Allied Mercantile Bank in southwest Houston and attempted to get a loan for $2500, using the two cars he held the title to as collateral. The loan was reportedly to be used as seed money for a business Robert wanted to start. The bank declined to loan them the money.

In the end, it was an anonymous caller that would lead investigators to Robert Lumas' whereabouts.

Women Were His Downfall

Sergeant Larry Ott and the others working this case were back on their regular shifts working new cases while still running down all possible leads in the Joyce Lumas murder. They talked with anyone who had known Robert Lumas, from old prison cell mates to old service buddies.

One day, Ott got a call from a female who said she had information regarding Robert Lumas' location. The woman refused to give her name but advised that Lumas was in Mexico, and that his mother spoke to him on a regular basis. Momma Lumas, however, did not speak to him from her home, but went to a friend's house where she made and/or received calls from her son. The anonymous caller gave Ott the phone number the calls were made both to and from. A subpoena was issued for telephone records for that number. In a few days, the records were secured, which indicated eight phone calls had been made both to and from Mexico.

Lumas was a native born American of Castilian Spanish descent, so extradition was not going to be a problem because the FBI has agents stationed in many foreign cities, including Mexico City. The local Houston FBI office had an older agent named Bob Lee, who was a hard charger with family ties inside Houston PD's detective bureau. Bob and his baby sister were both hard working cops and had each shot and killed people in the line of duty. His specialty was bank robberies. Bob got things rolling for the Homicide guys.

Lumas was arrested and placed in a Mexican federal judicial prison while awaiting extradition. On the morning of his extradition hearing, Mexico City was hit by a massive earthquake. Everything came to a complete standstill, and in the midst of the chaos, Lumas escaped from custody. When the home team was notified of his escape, they were dumbfounded. Every time they caught a break, something seemed to kick them in the teeth.

After several months, Robert Lumas was again arrested in sunny Mexico, while working on a relative's ranch. He was finally extradited back to Houston to stand trial, and once he was back in the Harris County jail, Dave Collier went to interview him. Lumas told Collier that on the day of the earthquake he escaped by crawling out of his cell via the jail ventilation system. He supposedly had been saving grease from his daily meal of chicken, which he stored in a tin can. He smeared the grease on his body in order to squeeze through the narrow air shaft system.

Lumas also told Collier that he had been arrested the second time because he pissed off a girlfriend he'd acquired during his stay there, who ratted him out in retaliation.

David Collier returned to Homicide from the Harris County jail and shared Lumas' statement with his fellow investigators. Collier thought it funny as hell that Robert Lumas was indicted based on testimony by a girlfriend he'd confided in, escaped, and was then arrested again in Mexico after telling his new sweet thing about his wanted status back in the states, and then pissing her off.

Robert Lumas ultimately entered a plea of guilty and was sentenced to forty years in prison. There was no affirmative ruling on Joyce Lumas' death having been caused by a deadly weapon. Hands and feet have now been affirmed as deadly weapons by courts of appeal regarding homicides therefore, if Joyce Lumas' hyoid bone (the small bone in the throat) had been recovered and found to be cracked, Robert Lumas would have faced a charge with a deadly weapon stipulation. Unfortunately, the hyoid bone is very thin, and was likely incinerated during her three cremations on Pelican Island. Lacking the deadly weapon stipulation, Lumas would only serve one quarter of his sentence (ten years) in prison before he was eligible for parole. He is currently walking the streets of Houston.

While out on parole, Lumas was arrested and charged with Aggravated Sexual Abuse of a Child. Charges were later dismissed, for reasons unknown—or understood—to me.

The actual evidence that brought about the murder charges against Lumas, and which would have convicted him had he gone to trial, were his own admissions. His confession to Mary Kroft- that he had murdered his wife and cremated her body-was admissible. His admissions to Aaron McFarland about burning a body and almost getting caught would have also been allowed into court as evidence.

One reason Lumas pled guilty was that he had other cases against him pending, including arson and robbery by assault. When he was charged and his photo appeared on TV and in the paper, one of his other victims recognized him and came forward. This woman had met Lumas at a bar where he charmed her and they left together. Lumas beat her up, robbed her of her purse and jewelry, and took her car. Then he torched her car.

In the words of the late Houston attorney Roy Bean, "Even a bass would not get caught if it kept its mouth shut." William Shakespeare is credited with the expression that "two men can keep a secret if one of them is dead." Robert Lumas' ego and mouth were what ultimately put him in prison the second time. Had he not gone into detail about his crime the only charge he likely would have faced would have been the misdemeanor charge of abuse of a corpse.

This was a "career case" for several investigators. Career cases are either a high point in a cop's career, or they twist your guts and leave a bad taste in your mouth every time you think of them. Some cases, such as this one, affect investigators in both ways.

There are two police expressions that hold true regarding this investigation. The first one is, "It is better to be lucky than good." The second comes from Captain Bobby

Adams of Houston's Homicide Division. Adams spent a total of forty years in Homicide, beginning as a detective, then as a lieutenant, and finally as a captain for well over twenty of those years. He would encourage his troops by saying, "Sometimes you make your own luck." That translates to, "Get off your butt–knock on doors, interview people and pass out business cards while you are wearing out shoe leather." A lot of cases get cleared by business cards. If the party you gave it to knows a witness he may (and often does) pass it along.

Captain Adams was impressed enough by the way the Joyce Lumas case was handled that he had a three-foot by three-foot poster made from a photograph taken of the cremation site from a Houston Police Department helicopter.

In part, the four investigators involved in this case made their own luck. The rest of their good fortune came about as a gift from elsewhere.

One final note: Robert Lumas went to prison believing he was still in line to receive Joyce's $350,000 life insurance payout. However, not only was Lumas not the beneficiary on Joyce's policy, but by law he would not have received life insurance benefits since he was convicted of her murder. So while this story had a happy ending for the investigators who worked tirelessly to solve Joyce's murder, it did not have a happy ending for Robert Lumas.

•JUST AN OLD SCHOOL YANKEE DIRTBAG•

The scene of this crime was less than a mile south of Houston's Galleria area in a high-end shopping center— a strip center that sat back about 150 feet from the street and covered a whole city block. At the west end of the one-story brick complex was a high-end dance club and bar, and a restaurant and bar at the other end. Almost directly between those two businesses was a high-end strip club.

There were several other businesses located in this particular shopping center, but only the three mentioned here were open late at night. Both the club and restaurant employed a pair of off-duty uniformed officers. The strip club, however, did not employ police officers because all Houston area police agencies prohibit off-duty officers from working security at sexually-oriented businesses. The club at the west end of the center had officers there seven nights a week, and the restaurant only on Friday and Saturday nights.

On the night of this incident, a Saturday night, the officers showed up at both businesses just before 10 p.m. One officer at each of the locations showed up a little early. Cops know that when it comes to being around people using alcohol, uniformed officers need to travel like nuns—always in pairs. Therefore both officers chose to stand on the sidewalk outside the front doors of their respective establishments and wait for that evening's partner. The cops stood between 250 to 300 feet apart. The matter that was about to hit the fan would never pass for roses.

First they heard muffled gunshots, and then the front plate glass window of the strip joint blew out. More gunshots—no longer muffled—came from inside the club. Men and women (some clad, others scantily clad) began running out of the front door, screaming. A couple of rounds had been fired after the front window glass shattered, followed by an almost eerie lull in the gunfire. As young uniformed officers are prone to do, both men ran into harm's way instead of first assessing the situation. Mark Crandall was through the door about four seconds ahead of Harry Womack. As Womack cleared the front door he heard a single round fired inside the club. As he entered the main part of the club from the foyer, Womack saw Crandall standing over a very dead man who was lying on the dance floor. In fact, Crandall had his foot planted on that man's right wrist. In the scumbag's hand was a cocked, silver-colored Colt pistol, held in a death grip. Mark Crandall had his duty weapon in hand, pointed at the chest of the man lying on the floor.

It was obvious to Womack that Crandall had scored a direct hit to the dead man's forehead, as the back of his head had blown all over the dance floor. Womack told Crandall, "It's okay Crandall, you got him. It's all over."

Crandall, never looking up, said, "I gotta make sure he doesn't move and nobody touches him." Womack responded, "I promise you he is not about to move or go anywhere. He is dead as hell, so put your pistol up and I'm gonna make sure nobody touches him."

Womack was a crime scene unit and had seen no end of dead people, but later confided in me that as he was looking at the stiff on the floor, he swore he'd seen smoke curling up from the bullet hole in the newly-rehabilitated dirt bag's forehead. It's funny what you focus on at the time and then go on to remember. When Crandall took his foot off the dead guy's wrist, Womack reached and snapped on the safety of the dead guy's cocked pistol. During his time as a crime scene unit he had seen more than one pistol discharge when some officer was trying to get it out of a dead or dying man's hand.

Employees from the club began coming out from behind the bar and out of back rooms where they had taken cover. They then began describing what led up to the fiasco.

The dead man was a lean and hard-looking guy, six foot tall, in his late fifties or early sixties and it was obvious that his hair had been dyed black. He was dressed in a black baggy suit and wore black Stacy Adams brand lace-up, pointed-toed shoes. You could tell he was expensively dressed, with a black neck tie and a starched white shirt. The kicker was that he wore white socks and his pants were too short–more commonly known as "high water" pants.

The now-dead guy had come into the club and ordered a couple of drinks, and was described by the waitresses as being both rude and snappy. The club employees immediately tagged him as being a Yankee (by his accent) and due to the fact he referred to a strip club as "a titty flop."

He reportedly was trying to pick up a stripper to take back to his hotel. He'd waved around a couple of hundred dollar bills but had no takers for the night. He ordered his third drink, and when the waitress brought it to him he pulled out a pistol and fired it at her, at almost point-blank range. Somehow he missed her. He then began randomly firing around the club as people screamed and scrambled for cover. When he ran out of bullets, the man put a fresh magazine in his pistol, grabbed a chair and moved out into the middle of the central wooden dance floor–just waiting. According to witnesses, Crandall came into the room and Mister Wonderful pointed his weapon at the officer. The rest, as they say, is history.

At any scene with a dead body, no one is supposed to touch the body until the medical examiner's office arrives. Well, someone ignored protocol and pulled the man's wallet out—then called the closest substation to run his Illinois driver's license to check his wanted status and criminal history. After that, they returned the wallet to the inside of the man's jacket pocket.

The license check set the computers afire, and the FBI was calling the Beechnut substation in a hurry. FBI agents and homicide detectives began arriving at the club in short order. The first thing everyone noted about the dead guy was his pistol. It was a highly engraved, nickel-plated weapon (later determined to come out of the Colt custom shop) and was what is called a commercial model. That means it was manufactured between WWII and 1970 and had the letter C in front of, or behind, its serial number. The weapon also had real (not plastic) mother of pearl grips, which are highly unusual.

The FBI wanted to take over the scene, but when asked when any of them had ever made a murder scene before, and which of them would present the matter to the Harris County District Attorney and grand jury, they opted to back off. At the scene, FBI agents never came out and said why they were so interested in the deceased, but sort of just blustered about. Communication with the FBI always seems to be like a one-way street, and goes their way only. Thankfully, other federal law enforcement agencies don't tend to behave the same way. Investigators never determined if the rehabilitated guy was under the witness protection program, or if there was another reason the FBI was so interested. It was obvious that he was a mob type. And now, his Welcome to Houston card had been officially punched, spindled and somewhat mutilated.

After the scene was processed it was noted the crook had a set of keys in his pocket with an odd key fob–yet not a factory type that unlocked car doors. The parking lots were full that night and one of the homicide detectives walked outside with the key ring. He punched the single button on the fob. One hundred feet from the club's front door, a car's driver side door unlocked as its motor started and the headlights lights came on. The vehicle was a Cadillac, about two years old, and clean as a new dime. It had dark tinted windows and an (ugly) aftermarket custom paint job that was green and black. The odd thing about the car was that the front end was jacked up about six inches higher than it should have been. The car was towed to the HPD print stall where it was gone over from front to back and even dope dogs were run past it. No contraband was ever found. Money the dead man had, class he did not.

It turned out that the mobster had some kind of designer drug in his system that he mixed with alcohol and Viagra, causing him to go off the deep end.

Other than the very deserving Yankee, the only other injury that night was to a bartender called Slim. He was shot through both cheeks of his buttocks about two inches north of the seat of his pants. The bullet ranged only through meat and hit neither bone or butt hole. Slim had been wandering around the scene with the rear end of his pants cut out and a pair of bandaged butt cheeks hanging out for all to see.

He kept saying, "He just shot me in the ass." He repeated this statement over and over again as the paramedics were trying to get him either to load up into their ambulance, or sign a waiver of service so they could get back to running more calls.

So, this story has a happy ending, but is not of bedtime quality that you could read to little children. The bent-nosed guy from Chicago went away forever and all the good guys in Houston lived happily ever after.

The End.

•THE RIGHT TO REMAIN SILENT•

This case had San Antonio, Texas in an uproar for several days as people searched for a kidnapping victim. A seething anger took its place thereafter. The defense attorney for the man ultimately charged said his client "was the most hated man in Bexar County" at his change-of-venue hearing—and he was right.

Here's the story.

Mary Morgan was a twenty-seven-year-old second shift registered nurse who got off duty around midnight. She was abducted from the parking lot of the Audie Murphy Memorial Veteran's Administration Hospital up on the north side of San Antonio. The hospital at the time was sort of out in the sticks, surrounded by a lot of pastures covered in mesquite. San Antonio is a major city but with a rather conservative population. One night, shortly after midnight, two people saw a black male–later identified as Sammy Tyrone Lawrence–speeding away from the parking lot where Mary Morgan's car had been parked. When she did not return home after work, her family contacted hospital security, who found her car in the lot and notified the San Antonio police. One witness was a security guard who gave the police the license number of the speeding car he had seen driving away from the lot where Mary's car was found.

This was a very good piece of police work by the San Antonio Police Department, moving on the case immediately. They figured out what had happened and took action rather than waiting until they had a victim. Their work in this matter is exemplary and it should be noted as such. Many major agencies would not have mobilized and done the immediate follow-up that is so critical in a case such as this.

The speeding car was registered to a convicted sex offender who had kidnapped and sexually assaulted a child in the past. In that case, he had been sent to prison and served about four and a half years of a ten-year sentence. Sammy Lawrence had only been out of prison for ten months when this particular kidnapping occurred. The police went to Lawrence's apartment (the address on his vehicle registration) and found him home. Interestingly enough, he had a pair of pants soaking in a pail of bloody water there in the front room. Personal items belonging to Mary Morgan were also found in a garbage can on the premises. The blood in the bucket from Lawrence's apartment would later be linked to the victim in this case. Lawrence was arrested from his apartment, and when read his legal warning, he invoked his right to remain silent. He knew his rights. He had been down this road before.

The case was picked up by both the local and national media and there were searches and investigations conducted. San Antonio's economy is based on several military posts and tourism, and many retired career military personnel live there. The whole town was upset. As hard as the police and citizens searched, Mary Morgan simply could not be located.

The detective assigned to this case was ultra-diligent. He and several others ran down clues and fielded the multiple phone calls that poured in daily. When his days off came, he continued to search for the victim on his own time. In fact, five days after Mary Morgan was abducted and raped, the detective personally found the victim, lying nude beside a fire ant mound in an open field two miles from the hospital where she had been abducted. When found, Mary was still alive, but just barely. It was summer in south Texas and hot as Hades. She had been stabbed seven times, and left for five days without water. Mary Morgan died the following day.

The twenty-two-year-old defendant's attorney won a change of venue due to the tremendous amount of news coverage in San Antonio. In fact, this case received news coverage throughout the nation. The trial was moved to Corpus Christi, Texas. A jury there had no trouble finding Lawrence guilty of capital murder and they sentenced him to death. That sentence was overturned upon appeal because the prosecution told the jury that Lawrence refused to talk to the police. His second trial took place in San Antonio and again he was convicted by a jury and sentenced to death. Four years later this misguided mother's son had his conviction overturned once more because the judge failed to include in his charge to the jury about the defendant's culpable mental state (whatever the hell that means). Lawrence's third trial took place two years later in Brownsville, Texas where, for the third time, this individual was convicted and sentenced to death. The sentence finally stuck, and thirteen years after taking the life of a decent person, the guilty party was put to death.

The irony in this case was pointed out to me by a Texas Ranger named Al Cuellar. Al said that due to the defendant in this case invoking his constitutional right to remain silent, he killed both Mary Morgan and himself. Her death was brought on by the advanced state of shock she suffered by being stabbed multiple times, as well as dehydration and exposure to the hot Texas summer sun. Had the defendant confessed and told investigators where he left his victim, he would never have received the death penalty because Mary would have physically recovered from her injuries. Investigators speculated that Lawrence thought Mary was dead when he left her lying in the field.

Lawrence was ultimately rehabilitated by the state of Texas in the only manner that works upon a sexual predator. This was a case of good police work where, sadly, the victim could not be found in time to save her life.

•I AIN'T GOT NO BODIES•

While researching another story that would come to be titled *No Human Involvement*, I spoke with Ted Wilson, who had been the prosecutor involved in that case. During our interview, he told me there was a somewhat similar (no body) case out of Medina County worked by a Texas Ranger named Trampas Gooding. Wilson teaches search-and-seizure cases around the state of Texas and met Gooding in a five-day class where he was instructing law enforcement officers. Ranger Gooding had an old double homicide case (fifteen plus years old) and he wanted to get a search warrant to search a piece of rural property for possible skeletal remains and DNA.

Wilson retired from the Harris County District Attorney's office and prior to retiring had worked as a special crimes prosecutor for many years. He was impressed by the work done by Gooding and told me the man's old case was well worth my looking into. I reached out to Gooding, and after he got a "He's okay and won't mess you over" phone call from another former Texas Ranger that I knew, Gooding called me.

When Texas Rangers get a new assignment or promotion they are often transferred to a new county or region of the state. Upon relocating, they inherit the old cases of their predecessors. For that matter, they also often get assigned to cases of other police agencies in the area, or counties they serve. Many murder cases they get are old, if not moldering. Rangers are also called into some fresh cases, often to oversee the investigation of area police shootings in small towns in the region within their jurisdiction. That way, someone from outside the agency can review the facts and there not be allegations of cover-ups or a biased investigation from within that favors the home team.

Ron "Trampas" Gooding is a Texas Ranger sergeant assigned to a cold case task force within the Texas Department of Public Safety. He was initially contacted about this murder case through the San Antonio Police Department.

The San Antonio PD Narcotics Division received word about a federal prisoner claiming to have information about a San Antonio drug dealer's murder. After ten or more months, the information was forwarded over to SAPD Homicide. Their cold case squad had a good working relationship with Gooding and the information finally got to him.

The inmate was sitting in a federal prison in Fort Worth, Texas, doing hard time for a methamphetamine conviction. His name was Henry Lozano and he wanted to pass on information regarding a fourteen- or fifteen-year-old murder case. Raymond Alexander (Alex) Molina and Andrea Denise Meaux had both been reported missing from San Antonio, Texas, but Lozano claimed to know that both Alex and Andrea were more than missing–they were dead as all get-out. Lozano knew all the players in this murder case, and was a wealth of information.

Alex Molina had run a dope transportation operation that ran drugs from Texas to Indiana. He was married to a woman named Kimbra, who was his second wife. Although married, Molina kept a stripper on the side whose name was Andrea Meaux. Multiple people were involved in Alex Molina's drug business. Among them were Daryl Bacon, Teresa "Terry" Valverde, Robert Gillespie, Ernesto Soto and Manuel Garza. Lozano met Soto through Bacon. Soto allowed Molina to store drugs in eighteen-wheeler trailers on his thirty-acre property near Natalia, in Medina County (west of San Antonio). Alex's drug dealing brought in a lot of money, but he was prone to living really far beyond his means and owed a lot of people money. In the drug business, beating people out of money or product is most often a death sentence. Molina supposedly owed Soto and Garza one hundred and sixty thousand dollars. Inside the drug culture, a debt that size justifies any murder. In fact, racking up a debt like that might be considered suicide.

People in the drug business will tell you that if someone steals from you, then you have to kill them. Otherwise, every other crook in town–and a whole bunch of junkies–will line up to be the next one to rip you off. It is nothing personal; it is just a part of doing business on any and all levels of the drug world. This is hard for Middle America to comprehend, but it is a fact of life where dopers live. It is a constant. The sun rises in the east and sets in the west–and if somebody rips you off, you have to kill them.

Lozano claimed that Soto told him about the murders of Alex Molina and Andrea Meaux. The killings occurred on Soto's home place in Medina County in the month of April. Soto admitted to Lozano that he shot and killed Andrea with a .22 pistol with one shot to the body, followed up by a bullet to the head. Manuel Garza (Soto's right hand in operations) was credited with shooting Alex. Both of the bodies were then buried on the property using a backhoe. Approximately six months after the murders, on Halloween night, Bacon and Lozano went to Soto's ranchito and dug up the bodies (again using the backhoe) and put the couple's remains atop a bonfire and cremated what had been two humans. Lozano claimed Soto kept a couple of souvenirs in the form of a belt buckle, a stone from a ring, and the firing pin from one of the guns used in the killings.

After taking Lozano's story, Trampas Gooding began interviewing the people Lozano mentioned to him. Daryl Bacon and Teresa Valverde–husband and wife–were first. Bacon said he had bought marijuana and methamphetamine from Lozano in the past and that he knew that Lozano was involved in some drug distribution deals with Soto and Garza. Terry Valverde was the ex-wife of Ernesto Soto, and Soto and her current husband, Daryl Bacon, were very good friends with Manuel Garza. Both Valverde and Bacon admitted having transported marijuana for Alex Molina in the past. Alex Molina was also Ernesto Soto's "primo hermano," meaning they were first cousins. They were a close family and their children had grown up together. However, blood relationships do not supersede the rules of the game in that business.

Bacon said he'd been told that Molina had shorted Soto and Garza a bunch of money and that a whole group of them had discussed what should be done to settle the account. Bombing Andrea Meaux's house, where Alex stayed regularly, was one option discussed. Robert Gillespie suggested using a paralytic drug he could steal from the hospital where he worked with Bacon. Terry Valverde admitted she was present when this conversation took place, but thought it was just a bunch of macho dopers blowing off steam, because everybody there was snorting methamphetamine that night. Soto ended the discussion by just saying not to worry about it because he was going to "take care of it."

Within a few days following this conversation, Soto contacted Bacon and asked him to pick up a couple of bags of lime and bring them to his property. Bacon told Gooding he knew the lime would be used on Andrea and Alex's bodies to speed up decomposition. Around a month and a half later, Soto reportedly called Bacon and told him that he'd shot a couple of bobcats out on his property. From that, Bacon understood that Alex and Andrea were no longer among the living.

Bacon admitted he was in the company of Henry Lozano on Halloween, after having picked up the two bags of lime for Soto. That day, Lozano and Bacon went to Soto's property and found Soto digging up Andrea and Alex's bodies with a backhoe. He put the remains on a big brush pile and doused it with gasoline before setting it ablaze. The men sat around talking and drinking that night, and the next morning Bacon found a turquoise belt buckle beside the fire pit and gave it to Soto. It was an unusual piece of silver jewelry with a wide-beveled outside edge. Soto told Bacon that he had shot Andrea and that his partner Manuel Garza had shot and killed Alex.

Soto then took his backhoe and ran it back and forth, grinding up all the charred bits of wood and ash with its tires and front-end loader bucket. Soto likely knew that extreme heat will destroy all DNA evidence. The cremation site was a trash- and brush-burning location that had been previously used for an undetermined amount of time, and would continue to be used for fourteen years before Gooding's investigation began.

On April 24th of the year in question, Terry Valverde admitted she told Soto she was going to visit her mother, who reportedly lived near Ernesto Soto's property. Soto asked her to call him if she saw Alex and Andrea on the road to his house. Valverde did, in fact, see the two while she was driving through LaCoste and she called Soto, like he had asked her to. Several months later Soto told Valverde that he and Garza had done away with Alex and Andrea. He claimed to have shot Andrea in the back of the head and said Garza had been the one who killed Alex.

Valverde and Bacon were charged with conspiracy to commit capital murder. Bacon agreed to plead guilty to the lesser crime of murder in exchange for a sentence that would not exceed twenty years. For this he agreed to testify truthfully against Soto and Garza at trial time. Charges against Valverde were dismissed shortly after their arrests. The State of Texas would later send Terry Valverde a letter saying that they had probable cause to believe she had committed the crime of conspiracy to commit capital murder. That letter also said that if she agreed to testify and cooperate by providing information in the case, she would not be prosecuted.

Gooding finally arrested Ernesto Soto and interrogated him for six hours straight. Once Soto was advised that his buddies in the dope business, including those who helped him burn the bodies, were lining up against him and telling everything they knew, Soto broke down and confessed. He claimed he killed Alex because Alex was reaching for a gun. He claimed he was forced to pull his own pistol and kill Alex in self-defense. Soto even went out to his property with the Gooding and walked around it, providing details of the killings which Gooding recorded on video.

When Manuel Garza was arrested he was not initially interested in making a statement. Ranger Gooding showed him the video of Soto talking about the shooting and Garza blurted out, "That son-of-a-bitch is the one that shot the woman, I'm the one who shot Alex." Garza was offered a deal to shore up the case against Soto. He agreed to plead guilty to a twenty-year sentence if he testified truthfully against Soto.

Armed with a search warrant, Gooding and six other Rangers arrived at Soto's property along with members of the Medina County Sheriff's Office, members of the FBI crime lab, and some staff members from North Texas State University's Forensic Science Department working under the direction of a Doctor Gill. There were also a group of volunteers that joined them at the scene. The group searched for six days, looking for a burial site and scouring the burn pit where the victims' remains were supposed to have been cremated. They also searched all structures–including the travel trailer Soto lived in, and the eighteen-wheel trailers used for storage.

The burial site was pretty well known, as Bacon and Gillespie had been there when the bodies were unearthed by Soto. Gillespie was of little to no help though, because by the time he was interviewed in Alpine, Texas, his brain was so fried (presumably from drug use) he was hard to even understand, and was therefore not be considered to be a credible and reliable witness. The burn pit site was a challenge, since it had been used for at least fifteen years. The whole of it, and the burial site, were dug up and the dirt sifted through screens. Investigators hoped to find some bones—no matter how small—to test for a DNA match. Both victims had family members, which meant even a small bone could be linked to either missing person. Often human teeth will survive a fire—not a professional cremation but one done on a wood fire such as this one.

The actual physical evidence linked to this case was sketchy at best. It consisted of a turquoise and silver woman's belt buckle and a loose diamond recovered from Garza's travel trailer. Garza denied they belonged to Andrea. Pictures produced by some of Andrea's family members showed her wearing a belt buckle just like the one recovered. Bacon testified the buckle looked just like the one he found by the cremation pit that he had given to Soto. The admissions by the defendant to persons close to him (like an ex-wife), and from his admitted co-conspirator, Manual Garza, were what really sunk Soto. In the drug world, however, it was necessary for Soto and Garza to get the word out about killing the thief and his kept woman. It was how good drug dealers took care of business. The follow-up was equally important– getting the word out that such behavior would not be allowed. The penalty for violators was death. No trial, no questions asked. This protocol bolsters their positons in the illicit pharmaceutical community.

The capital murder trial of Ernesto Soto took place in Hondo, Texas, which is the county seat of Medina County. Judge Mickey Pennington presided over the trial and District Attorney Daniel Kindred prosecuted. At the time of his trial, Soto was fifty-three years old and Rodriquez was fifty-seven. When murdered, Andrea Meaux was twenty-nine and Alex Molina was forty-two.

Soto was represented at trial by an attorney named Martin Underwood, who had a reputation as a good criminal trial lawyer. He was reputed to try cases in one of two ways. The first was by attempting to get a not guilty verdict. His second common strategy was to try to have his client's sentence overturned on appeal due to some sort of reversible error being admitted into the trial.

Henry Lozano admitted being present during the digging up of the cadavers and the burning of their skeletal remains. He also covered the admissions made to him by Soto about who he and Garza killed and how the killings had taken place. Lozano, at the time of his testimony, had been released from federal custody and enjoyed a whole month of freedom before he was arrested for possession of methamphetamine. He was already in a Texas state prison when he took the stand as a witness in Medina County.

Daryl Bacon and Teresa Valverde testified as to their knowledge and their relationships with both Soto and the dead man, Alex Molina. They admitted their involvement in the world of drug transportation and distribution as well as their own personal drug use. The fact that Bacon was testifying in order to get a sentence not to exceed twenty years was also disclosed. The fact that Terry Valverde had been charged with conspiracy to commit capital murder and charges had been dismissed if she would testify truthfully against her former husband. The state's witnesses included quite a cast of characters, but the best was yet to come.

What really sank Soto was the testimony of his partner in crime, Manuel Garza. He testified that on the day of the murders he arrived at Soto's property in the late afternoon. Soto, Alex and Andrea were already there. He was introduced to Andrea but he already knew Alex from prior dealings. He said that they all snorted some methamphetamine, although Alex did not partake because he was feeling very ill. Alex apparently suffered from medical problems related to having both diabetes and issues with cirrhosis of the liver. Garza said he left his travel trailer and went to check the mail. He came back in approximately five minutes and found that Alex and Soto were gone.

Andrea was still in the travel trailer and said the two other men had gone down to the eighteen wheeler trailers to look at a load of marijuana. Garza knew there was no weed in the trailers and he got on his all-terrain vehicle and made the short run down to the storage facilities. When he arrived, he found the two men, but Alex was really sick and asked Garza to go get his medicine and Andrea, and bring them both back. When Garza got back to the travel trailer, Andrea had a pistol out and pointed it at him, asking him if he had heard a gunshot. He said no and told her he'd returned because Alex was feeling really sick and wanted him to get her and his medicine. Her survival skills kicked in, so she marched Garza down to the trailers ahead of her at gunpoint. He told her to calm down and took out his own gun and put it on the hood of a truck to show he was not a threat to her. At that she walked on ahead of him, and when they reached the storage trailers they found Alex lying on the ground and Soto standing nearby. Garza said Andrea turned back toward him, with her gun still in her hand, and he shot her in the body with the .22-caliber backup pistol he carried in his hip pocket. She fell to the ground and moaned. Soto walked up to where she lay and shot her one time in the head. Garza further testified that he and Soto got the backhoe and dug a hole with it, then put the two bodies in the hole and poured lime atop the cadavers—to speed up decomposition—then covered the remains with dirt.

After burying the bodies, the two men disposed of Andrea's car. Garza drove it to San Antonio where they abandoned it in a parking lot, leaving the keys in the ignition. Their hope was that it would be stolen, further confusing the trail if any investigation that might follow. Garza also admitted he was testifying to earn him a twenty-year sentence for the reduced charge of murder.

The jury was charged with their responsibilities and sent off to deliberate. They were outside of the courtroom for a whole thirty minutes before they returned with a verdict. During that time period they picked a foreman, voted as to the defendant's guilt or innocence, and filled out the required paperwork for the court. Capital murder in Texas has a minimum life sentence attached to any conviction, and the presiding judge sentenced Soto accordingly.

Manuel Garza pled guilty to a murder charge and was sentenced to twenty years. He died in prison of natural causes approximately three years to the date of his arrest in this case. Daryl Bacon pled guilty to a conspiracy to commit capital murder charge and got less than half of the maximum sentence he'd originally agreed to.

Trampas Gooding is still Rangering in the counties around San Antonio. He has received a lot of accolades for his investigation into this old and moldering case. He gave much of the credit for the convictions to the work of Daniel Kindred, the district attorney of Medina County. He also said the case just fell together well as he interviewed the parties involved. Had the suspects refused to talk to him the investigation would have ended with a convicted drug felon in a federal prison telling a story.

There are expressions in police work that are appropriate here. One is, "It is better to be lucky than good." Another is, "You make your own luck." I'd like to submit a third: "Sometimes you clear a case you shouldn't, and at other times you know who did it and you can't buy a break at any price." In my opinion, this case was solved and the suspects were convicted because of both good fortune and a whole lot of good police work.

•DEATH OF A LAWMAN•

Author's Note: This story is written in the first person, because that is how it was related to me by the game warden familiar with this case. The facts were researched and verified before being included in this book.

Ronnie Germany and I went through the Texas State Game Warden's Academy in 1971. After completing our training, he was assigned to San Augustine County and I was sent to Tyler County, both in eastern Texas. I'd been raised in San Angelo out in west Texas. I am here to tell you that East Texas was a real culture shock for me in so many ways. I'd never been around alligators or a bunch of inbred snuff dippers who had only worn shoes when they either joined the Army or were getting married. This is a part of the state called the Big Thicket and I swear to you that they have to pump daylight back into some parts of that country. It was not unusual to run up on people living in what passed for a house that had dirt floors. Moonshiners were not uncommon either.

Game wardens in rural counties are not just "possum cops" but get involved in every phase of law enforcement throughout the state. We back up other law enforcement officers and they do the same for us. Some of those really rural counties do not have much of a tax base and there may be a total of fifteen sworn officers inside the whole county. When you take those fifteen and split them into two or three shifts, and factor in days off, the thin blue line gets stretched even thinner. Some little towns have no city police and the sheriff's department is supposed to take care of everything. When you are out on patrol you may well be there "all on your lonesome." Game wardens regularly run up on whiskey stills, automobile chop shops, meth labs and marijuana growing operations. It's not unusual for them to get involved in manhunts, chasing fugitives, and working murders with the local constabulary.

The fall hunting season brings out hordes of people with high-powered rifles and shotguns, and in my experience, many of them were at least half drunk the bulk of the time. Game outlaws were common and night hunting of deer–and hunting them with dogs–is still a way of life for many of the unwashed. A lot of backwoods people were loggers. Probably eighty-five percent of the pulp wood loggers (pronounced pup-wood) in 1971 through 1973 were black males who resembled professional wrestlers. You were lucky to get your handcuffs to click one time on their wrists. Rough and tumble was the normal way of life with a lot of the folks you dealt with.

At the time, police car radios were low frequency units and everyone was on the same channel. You could talk to and hear other agencies in adjoining towns if you were not in a low or dead spot. In fact, several agencies would use their radios to communicate rather than spend money on a long distance phone call. If you were out of communication with the area troops, things could get dangerous in a hurry. To the locals you were not a game warden; you were "one of them laws." If you had a badge and a gun you were all lumped into that same group. If Mother Teresa had worn a badge and a gun she would have been included in that classification.

On July 29, 1973, Ronnie Germany was twenty-six years old and had been a warden for only about eighteen months. He was assigned to show a brand new rookie warden, Bill Decker, the ways of the world. Ronnie was driving around in the Attoyac (pronounced Toyack by the locals) river bottoms with the new boy on the block, stopping to visit with land owners. The Attoyac River separates San Augustine and Nacogdoches counties. The two wardens drove up to a shotgun house that was up on blocks and pretty well devoid of paint. There was a sixty-three-year old white male named Bernice Parish who was out in the yard tending to his garden. When "the laws" stepped out of their car, Parish ran through the front door, into his house. The two wardens were kind of dumbstruck by his actions and just stood there and looked at one another in disbelief.

Suddenly, Parish reappeared in the open front door and began firing a .22 rifle at the two men. Ronnie was hit one time in the chest. He and Decker began returning fire. East Texans were (at that point in history) not much impressed by handguns. When you pulled out a shotgun or rifle, however, you tended to get taken more seriously. The two wardens exchanged gunfire with Parish, and Ronnie told his rookie to take the state car and drive about a mile and a half down the road to where a deputy lived. Ronnie must not have thought he was all that badly injured, and in hindsight, it was not a good move to separate from his partner. Decker did as he was told.

The deputy was able to hit a radio tower and get the assist rolling. Parish must have gone out of the back side of the house after Decker drove off. Two wardens in Nacogdoches County were just across the river and beat the deputy and Decker back to the scene. They found Ronnie dead on the ground in the yard beside the house.

Investigators speculated Ronnie saw or heard Parish exit the house via the back door, and it appeared Ronnie was flanking the house when he collapsed. Parish then approached and shot Ronnie one more time between the eyes. An autopsy would show Ronnie also suffered a skull fracture from being hit with a blunt object–consistent with a gun barrel having struck him. The medical examiner testified that the .22 bullet fired into Ronnie's skull was done so with the gun in direct contact, or loose contact, to his head. It was obvious the shooter's intent was not to get away before fatally shooting Ronnie.

The manhunt was on. All available lawmen drew into the area, and mounted Texas Department of Corrections (now Texas Department of Criminal Justice) prison guards and their man-trailing hounds were called in.

Bernice Parish was a tenant farmer and a woodsman. He was reported to always travel armed. He was known to supplement his income by seeking and harvesting wild herbs and roots. His specialty was one called snakeroot. He also trapped during the fur season. It was determined that his murderous actions were motivated by the fact he had a barrel of sour mash percolating (rotting) inside his house. The most common product used to make the base for moonshine was unprocessed chicken feed. Processed chicken feed, when used as a base, will throw off chemicals that can poison or blind people. Anyone who has ever seen moonshine made (or the conditions it is made under) would never drink it.

Parish was trailed to the river by the dogs and he swam

across and ran parallel to the river for a ways and then crossed it again. He repeated this tactic several times. Any woodsman would know that raccoons use the same tactics when being trailed by hunting hounds. Here he was attempting to elude the dogs and the mounted prison guards. The search with the dogs was called off as daylight ran out.

As night closed in, the lawmen in the area of the house were pulled back and the around-the-house perimeter was pulled back. Two deputies with shotguns remained inside the darkened house. About two in the morning, their suspect returned to his home and entered through the back door. The deputies called out for him to surrender. Parish dove off the back porch as he was fired upon. He was uninjured but the hip pocket of his overalls (pronounced overhauls among the unwashed) was struck with a load of buckshot and a pair of gloves therein was blown to doll rags. Parish hit the ground running and took off through the woods again. Some distance away he ran out onto a road and was illuminated by the headlights of a state trooper's car. He stopped, threw his hands into the air and surrendered.

When Bernice Parish was arrested there was a brand new rookie state trooper with the Texas Rangers who took him into custody. Later, I asked the Ranger why he had not just shot and killed the suspect. He said under different circumstances he might well have, but he did not know how the rookie would react.

At the time of Ronnie's murder there was no capital murder law in Texas, as it had been struck down by the Supreme Court as cruel and unusual. The charges available were murder with malice of forethought, and murder without malice of forethought. The statute *without forethought* (which carried a two- to five-year sentence) was thought to cover situations like a bar fight when someone gets hit with a chair and dies from blunt trauma to the head. The *with forethought* statute was intended to cover premeditated murder and carried a sentence of no less than five, or more than ninety-nine years, or life.

In the time period leading up to Ronnie's killer's murder trial, there was a lot of racial tension in San Augustine County. There had been three police shootings within about a six-month period. The first was when two Texas Department of Public Safety troopers shot a black motorcyclist who pulled out a derringer during a traffic stop. The second was a situation where a mental case who was sitting on his porch began shooting at passing cars. "The laws" were called and when a patrol car pulled up, the man would run out and shoot at the officer with a shotgun. He wounded a state trooper, an EMT, and both the sheriff and his chief deputy. The man was firing birdshot–or what was known as squirrel shot in east Texas-at "the laws." This usually consisted of #2 to #4 birdshot. Both the chief deputy and sheriff lost an eye that day before that suspect was killed. The third shooting was Ronnie's murder.

When the case came to trial there were eight black and four white jurors. They found Bernice Parish guilty of murder with malice of forethought and sentenced him to five years in prison. The law enforcement community was both astounded and outraged. Ronnie was survived by a wife and had no children.

This was the first police funeral I ever attended. I don't know if the funeral home couldn't putty up the hole between Ronnie's eyes or what the problem was, but they simply put a Band-Aid over the bullet hole in his forehead. That always struck me as somewhat odd. It's kinda funny what sticks in your brain after all these years.

Unfortunately I attended too many other such funerals. The hostility toward law enforcement officers in those years was all too common. The rookie game warden who had been with Ronnie that day (Bill Decker) drowned seventeen years later during a bitterly cold search-and-rescue m–ssion on a lake in Panola County, Texas. The game warden that was with Decker on that mission was named Bruce Hill, and he also drowned when the boat they were in hit a stump about ten o'clock at night and flipped over.

•BLACK TAR•

There are a few constants in the drug world. One of them is that if you are in the dope business one of two things is bound to happen to you: you will either go to jail or get killed. It may be that both will occur. Those two options are simply occupational hazards that are part of the illegal pharmaceutical business. (Yet not hazards covered under OSHA.) Many people in this vocation operate with the mentality that they should live fast, die young and make a good-looking corpse.

Mid-level narcotics units in police agencies are always looking for the major league dealers. Five- or twenty-pound marijuana deals are of little significance. To get to the bigger cases (bigger dealers) you need good informants. Snitches on this level are not school kids who can put you onto a knuckle dragger who sells a couple of ounces of weed from behind a local convenience store. The valuable informants are medium-sized dogs that run with a big dog pack. Many of these operations–the big dog packs–are run by ex-convicts affiliated with prison gangs like the Mexican Mafia or the Texas Syndicate. In larger drug investigations, cops will arrest a lot of people who want to work off their cases by leading police to a larger fish. You use smaller fish to catch the big ones, although most of the offers made by crooks wanting to become informants are culled for one reason or another.

These eager-to-please crooks all want police to "put them on the street" so they can produce. The best informants are mercenary people who want to make money off helping put people from their own social circles in jail. Many police officer-informant relationships can go on for several years. This is not to say that the informant has given up the dope business; in most cases, he or she has not. The person who will know who is dealing what, or when major shipments arrive at a drug stash house will not be a choir boy or psalm singer. In this crowd, it's common to hear, "You can't be trusted until you've done hard time." They are usually close associates of dealers in the big leagues.

Frank Scoggins worked in a mid-level narcotics unit out of the Houston Police Department. Frank was an adrenaline junkie whose life ambition was to drive a race car in the Indianapolis 500. Just in case they ever called needing him to fill in for someone, Scoggins chose to practice his driving skills everywhere he went. If you told Frank he was cutting it pretty close while weaving in and out of traffic on some freeway he was likely to tell you that, "A lesser man would have been killed." He was a tall guy who sported a handlebar mustache and a lopsided grin. He'd also been stopped for speeding by at least half of the state troopers in the state of Texas. As a patrolman he had gotten special training in drug interdiction and made one of the largest cocaine busts in Houston police history while in uniform and driving a marked patrol car.

When he made it to the mid-level unit he figured he had found Valhalla, the heaven that Norsemen went to when killed in battle. Narcotics issued him an AR-15 rifle and a Benelli shotgun with a 14-inch barrel. That scattergun would fire so fast that he could have all seven fired hulls in the air at one time. Though the man was not Army sniper trained, he did qualify with iron sights on an M-16 at 500 meters. He set his deer feeders at three hundred meters, "Because you see so much more that way." Frank would go on to become the point man on a Narcotics entry team, among other things.

Houston's mid-level narcotics unit was one that hit drug operations fast and furious. Its very nature was to run and gun, hitting drug sites hard and fast, to take down the crooks in a hurry. Keeping the cops assigned to the unit safe was always the first priority. The officers there came away from some locations without drugs, but did not worry about "hitting a dry hole." Their orientation was that you just keep moving and work your cases, all the while putting crooks in jail. They also worked at keeping their informants safe. Warrant writing was such that you needed to get the proper information on paper to have a judge sign it. The wrong wording or too much information would get your information source killed. Informants can be replaced, but reliable ones are like gold.

The amount of black tar Mexican heroin coming into Texas at times is staggering. When there was an oversupply on the market, mid-level dealers would go to a wholesaler to buy. If they were looking to score an ounce they might be given two ounces and told to have their payment back in four days. Street dealers often had two or three balloons of smack in their mouth (so they could swallow it if confronted by the cops) and twenty in their underwear. The skills required to be a street level vendor of illegal drugs does not include having a high IQ.

One of my favorite ploys that the narcs used at times was the pay phone argument. A lot of barrio grocery stores still have pay phones hanging on the walls outside the building. Street drug dealers would walk back and forth on the sidewalk in front of the store. The narcotics officer would get on the pay phone and get into a conversation with a non-existent person until the dealer got close. Often times, anyone listening thought the guy on the phone was arguing with his wife. When the dealer walked within striking range, the cop would then grab him by the throat and choke him down until he spat out his dope-filled balloons. The logic of hiding other balloons in your jockey shorts is completely illogical to me, but there again, shooting drugs in your veins makes no sense to me either. Once captured, the street vendor would often lead cops to his home or stash location when asked him where it was. These guys are then pumped for information and flushed away into the system.

Frank had a confidential informant buying dope for him in northeast Houston, in order for Frank to procure a warrant. The CI came back with a quarter ounce and said the broker he was dealing with had bragged about buying nine ounces of uncut dope. Frank and company sat up on the location and waited for their crook to come out of his house. It did not take long before their dealer pulled out of his house with his wife and kid in the car with him. They had a uniformed unit stop the dealer's car on traffic. Their crook, Sergio Gomez, was Mexican Mafia connected and did not want to go back to prison. He was an habitual criminal who knew any further convictions would earn him a life sentence.

When questioned, Gomez told Frank he got his dope out of San Antonio and bought at least nine ounces of high-quality black tar at a time. He said the drugs were so pure that he could step on it (cut it with filler) pretty hard and make some really good money. Gomez was charged and put in jail with a *no bond* because he was on parole for dealing drugs. A short time later, Gomez decided he wanted to play ball and signed a contract with the district attorney's office to get a "get out of jail free card," as it is called.

Gomez was locked down in the Harris County Jail. A deal was set up with his San Antonio connection named Flaco. Frank had cleared it with his lieutenant to buy and walk away with nine ounces of heroin in order to identify the major league guy and get lined up with a mother lode of dope. The dope business is rather fluid, so you have to be able to adapt as the events change. Frank got with a San Antonio police officer named Doug Wilson who was the SAPD liaison with the state police narcotics unit. He was the go-to guy if you needed to get a helicopter or the Fifth Army to help you run warrants in Bexar County, or the entire south Texas area, for that matter. It was game on for the home team to take Gomez to make his nine-ounce buy from the dealer known as Flaco.

Frank and company checked Gomez out of the county jail and headed west to the Alamo City. The deal went as planned and Flaco showed up at the designated spot, a car wash. The deal went down and Gomez got nine ounces of high purity dope. The posse followed Gomez's source back to his house on the west side of San Antonio. From the location of the house, a license plate number and his alias, SAPD was led to believe that Flaco was a Mexican Mafia member whose real name was Eloy Mata. Doug Wilson pulled up a copy of Mata's driver's license and Gomez made a positive ID of Mata as being the man he knew only as Flaco–the man from whom he'd just purchased dope.

Ten days later, the second nine-ounce buy was set up between Gomez and Flaco. Like before, Gomez had an audio sender, or "wire," hidden in his billed cap. The transaction was made and Eloy Mata was followed home as before. SAPD sat up on the house where the heroin seller lived, which was located on a dead end street. The SAPD troops had only been set a few minutes when Flaco drove away from the house, and SAPD stopped him with a marked police car. Mata, aka Flaco, was told police were in the process of obtaining an arrest warrant for him along with a search warrant to go after dope at his house.

Eloy Mata saw the writing on the wall at once and opted to try and play *let's make a deal.* He signed a consent-to-search and went back home with the cops. There they found ten and a half pounds of black tar heroin in his home. This was an unheard-of amount of this drug to be found in one spot. Their suspect was more concerned with the fact that there were some stolen guns in his house than being caught with the dope. Frank told him to forget about the guns. Mata said his source kept his dope buried on his ranch, twenty-five to forty miles south of San Antonio, and said the dealer often kept twenty-five to fifty pounds of the stuff on hand. This ranch, Mata claimed, was the Mexican Mafia's main distribution hub. Frank had visions of snagging an even bigger load of dope and maybe even a ranch. Mata was run past a federal magistrate for a legal warning and he remained adamant about wanting to work a deal with the Feds.

The DEA Special Agent in Charge (SAC), however, was not interested in moving forward quickly to bring down a major criminal organization. To pull it off, they were going to have to move in a hurry. Both the Texas state and federal government's narcotics teams have very strict rules and act like they are bound so tightly to these rules that they don't, or can't, make changes on the fly as drug deals progress. It's like they are either very anal retentive or constipated all the time.

Also, with both agencies, if you make a run at a crook and come up empty on your search warrant then it looks bad on your record, and to come up empty too often can stall or quash your chances for promotion. Success, however, will help you moving up the ladder if you have the foresight and brass to do the job right and trust your men. The DEA's agent in charge also said he did not want to deal with Houston Narcotics because of their reputation for being loose cannons and a bunch of cowboys.

Though the Feds have the manpower, funds and equipment, many believe that they worry a lot about what the home office will think if they come up empty on a potential big operation. To have a dry run or two every now and then is expected, but some organizations want a sure thing that will get them honors and accolades.

At last, the ranch was run on with a warrant, but it was a pretty long time after the fact. Eloy Mata was stuck in the Bexar County jail and that black tar operation had, for the most part, relocated. Agents and dogs were run past the location and the whole of the property was searched. No quantities of dope were found or seized.

The only items found were a machine used to bag dope up in one-pound airtight bags, and some bags with drug residue in them, all found on a burn pile on the property. With this evidence alone, the federal conspiracy to commit law was used to charge several people and seize the property in question. Housekeeping in these operations should be a major concern, but it is hard to get good help. After the warrant was run it was determined that no fewer than three—and maybe more–people connected to this Mexican mafia operation were killed on the US side of the river.

It says in the Good Book that the wages of sin are death. Similarly, if you are considered a possible weak link in a drug operation, you and any other suspected possible snitches will be eliminated. Sadly, there does not have to be any real proof to support a supposition that a person is an informant. At least this was a story with a happy ending in the world of police work. The only sad part is that as soon as one player is rehabilitated (killed), another is waiting in the wings to take his place. The lure of easy money and a life in the fast lane is too strong.

A short time after the Mata heroin arrest, Doug Wilson of SAPD was saved by his ballistic vest. He was the entry man into a west side San Antonio home. Just as he entered the front door he was shot with a shotgun. The vest saved his life, and Wilson rehabilitated his assailant with his duty weapon. The dead suspect's family went before the media claiming the dead man did not know the narcotics team were policemen. A police department spokesman came on television with Wilson's ballistic vest. The whole shot pack had hit his vest right in the O of the word POLICE stenciled across the front of the vest. Internal Affairs never even looked into the allegation.

•OFFICER DOWN—SHOTS FIRED•

This is a hard story for me to tell, much less write about. It tends to bring out the dark side in me. It includes two mad-dog killers, two drunks who were homicide investigators, and one low-life individual who is still a highly-touted criminal defense attorney in Houston. I knew the investigators who worked the case and the clans from which the suspects came. The big wheel attorney hired by the suspect's family is a man I have dealt with a few times, but only ever knew him in passing. This was an open-and-shut case that got mucked up by the two incompetents assigned to it, and by an attorney who was (and still is) among the lowest of the low. I still ponder the question about who was the sorriest excuse for a human being (other than the robbers turned killers) involved in this whole matter.

Martin Barry was a Harris County Deputy Sheriff. He was married, had two kids, and his daughter was in her second year of college. He and his wife Lisa had planned their lives as best they could for their family. Family was everything. They even had their two children five years apart so that they could afford to put them both through college. Paying for out-of-town college was not in the cards, but the kids could go to college locally and work part-time. They were thrifty people who lived in a middle class neighborhood in Pasadena, Texas. They never bought a new car, and tried to make their cars last five to eight years before purchasing a new used car. Martin worked day shift in the county jail, and like most cops, worked off-duty security jobs at night to make ends meet. He also took his lunch to work in order to save money. One of the extra duty jobs he worked was closing a pizza parlor on Houston's southwest side, a job he worked Friday and Saturday nights.

One Friday night, just before 10 p.m., the restaurant crowd was thinning out and closing time was in sight. The employees had started their closing routine and only a few diners still remained in the restaurant. About nine fifty, two black males in their mid-twenties walked in the door. Martin was in uniform and standing up by the front register. Security personnel in these settings tend to function like a scarecrow to keep the bad guys away. The objective is to shoo them away to somewhere else.

That, unfortunately, did not happen on this particular evening. The two men, Andre Doucett and Johnny Ray Stamford, strolled on in and walked up to the uniformed officer. Without saying a word, Doucett shot Martin Barry in the head with a .357 Magnum revolver at almost point-blank range. The cashier began to scream hysterically and Johnny Ray ran up to the deputy and grabbed his gun out of his holster.

The restaurant manager, Irving Harris, came out of the back office with his own .357 Magnum revolver in hand. He immediately shot and killed Andre Doucett and then turned his attention toward Johnny Ray Stamford. He fired at Johnny Ray, and Johnny Ray returned fire. Harris was shot in the abdomen and knocked off his feet. Stamford ran from the scene with the dead deputy's weapon in his hand. The *assist the officer – officer down* call dropped and the Fifth

Cavalry arrived, but they were too late to either save a good guy, or send the second bad guy on a one-way trip to Hades. Irving Harris was severely wounded, but he fortunately survived.

Uniformed cops held the scene after the EMTs declared Martin and Doucett dead. The blue suits moved all the witnesses into the dining area, away from the bodies. They kept the gawkers out, and called Houston Homicide. There was no end of people, police cars and news vehicles gathering in the parking lot. Homicide sent a pair of night shift detectives, Albert Harmon and John Thorn, to the scene. Another detective named Ken Sloan was sent to Ben Taub Hospital to attempt to interview the wounded manager before he was taken into surgery.

A major from the Sheriff's Department showed up before the Homicide duty lieutenant and detectives arrived. He demanded to see Martin's body but was denied entry into the building. He got loud and tried to intimidate the officer minding the door. He was advised he was impeding the investigation, and if he continued he would be arrested. The major had been given the name and badge number of the deputy, but was told that until he (the city officer) was given orders to do otherwise by some honcho from Homicide, nobody was entering the building. The major asked the officer if he physically thought he could keep him out of the scene. The County Mountie was told that if he tried to get past the officer that he would be put on the ground, handcuffed, and put into the back seat of a patrol car. At this, the major stomped off to his car and drove away. He was, in his mind, a real somebody and called the Houston Police Department chief's office the next day. After he carried on for a few minutes, the sergeant who took his call was not impressed much either and told the angry major that their officers did everything right. After dealing with Major Somebody the sergeant found out the name of the uniformed officers who dealt with that official and put them in for a commendation for handling the scene properly.

Detective Ken Sloan was able to visit with the wounded restaurant manager in the hallway of the emergency room of Ben Taub Hospital. Irving Harris told Ken he'd been sitting in his office doing paperwork and heard a single gunshot. He grabbed his revolver and went into the front of the restaurant. He could see Martin Barry on the floor near the register and two armed black men near him. Harris said he fired first at the man nearest the register and then at the man nearest the downed deputy. The second man he shot at returned fire and Harris was knocked off of his feet.

While Harris was being interviewed (lying on a gurney while awaiting surgery), a black male on another gurney was rolled past where the manager and detective were talking. Harris pointed to the man being wheeled past and said, "And that's the second son-of-a bitch that I shot at and who shot me." The man on the gurney was Johnny Ray Stamford.

Stamford was in fact also suffering from a gunshot wound but refused to let the hospital staff remove the bullet lodged in his abdomen. He claimed he had accidentally shot himself and would not produce details of the shooting incident or the weapon. He knew that, as an ex-con, he could go to prison for possession of a firearm. Further, if the bullet removed was proven to be from Harris's gun, he would be guilty of robbery/homicide. Unfortunately, Stamford recovered from his injury without any further complications, nor a need for surgery. The restaurant manager got a secondary infection and darned near died from his wound.

Detective Ken Sloan filed capital murder charges

against the suspect Stamford that night, and Stamford was put into the county jail ward there in Ben Taub Hospital. Doucett was sent to the Harris County morgue for processing. The bullet removed from his worthless carcass during autopsy would be identified as having come from Irving Harris' Ruger Security Six. The bullet that killed Martin Barry came from a stolen revolver recovered from the floor next to Doucett's body.

Detectives Thorn and Harmon worked night shift and made murder scenes, processed prisoners and took statements. They did not do the follow-up investigations on cases, and therefore the deputy sheriff's murder case was passed on to two dayshift sergeants. Unfortunately the two sergeants–John Douglas and Darren Biggs–were drunken pieces of trash who also happened to be policemen. I do not know of Douglas' background. But before he was promoted to sergeant, Darren Biggs was a screw-up as a patrolman and seemed to rotate about once a year into the Jail Division after some supervisor had enough of him. Douglas would live to be eighty proof before he passed on to the big distillery in the sky.

The suspect Doucett lived in southeast Houston in a part of town called Sunnyside. Stamford lived in northwest Houston in a neighborhood called Acres Homes. Both were blighted areas that you would avoid if you had any snap and knew what is good for you. The morning after the murder, the dead deputy's pistol showed up on a front porch three doors down from the Doucett family home. The residents there called it in as found property and it was immediately noted that the gun had a silver butt plate with the dead man's name and badge number on it. With the discovery of the murder victim's weapon and the fact it was found on the opposite side of town from where Stamford lived, the two hot-shot detective-sergeants assigned to the follow-up investigation ruled Stamford out as a suspect in the killing of Deputy Barry. Their logic was based on their premise that a north side black man and a south side black man would not be running together. On top of that, the murdered policeman's gun had been recovered just down the street from the dead suspect's family home.

The two dayshift aces muddied up the report pretty well with their faulty assumptions. Then, two weeks after the killing, one of Houston's higher-priced defense attorneys walked into Homicide with a man in tow that he claimed was the one who shot the restaurant manager. That alleged suspect was a man named Jimmy Bench. Bench lived in what had been Doucett's neighborhood and gave a confession, knowing the facts of the case. He said he wanted to clear the matter up because an innocent man was facing charges that should have been his. Biggs and Douglas took the audio confession from the slow-witted suspect. Bench admitted being in on the robbery, and shooting at the white guy with the gun one time after Doucett got shot. He said he then ran away. The new suspect was put in jail and the two investigators presented the case to the Harris County District Attorney's office. Bench was charged with aggravated robbery and capital murder of a police officer. Jimmy Stamford was released from the county jail a couple of days later and the two drunks/detectives now had bragging rights. They'd gotten the real killer and cleared the case.

Their bragging rights lasted no more than three weeks. Then the court-appointed attorney who was assigned to defend the alleged murder and robbery suspect Jimmy Bench dropped a mega-ton bomb in Homicide's lap. It seems Jimmy Bench could not have been involved in the robbery and homicide at the restaurant because he had, at the time of the murder, been a ward of the state and was housed in the Rusk State Mental Hospital in eastern Texas. Jimmy Bench's bogus charges were dropped and a murder suspect got away unscathed, except for the bullet in his abdomen for which he got free medical treatment at a county charity hospital.

If there was any justice in this case, however, it is that the killer of Deputy Martin Barry was himself killed that night by an honorable man. Barry left behind two children and a wife. One of the drunken sergeants is dead after he was consumed by his own liver. The other sot of an investigator still has to live with himself. Unfortunately, the suspect that got away is still on the streets and gets to brag about his involvement in this murder case and beating the system. A couple of years after the killing it was determined that Jimmy Stamford and Andre Doucett were in fact first cousins. I guess a north side black and a south side black *can* have a connection and run together. Hopefully someday the two cousins and a certain attorney will share a pit in Hell for eternity.

•THE TUNNEL RAT•

Before the Vietnam War ended, it was determined that the North Vietnamese had constructed many of their permanent jungle compounds underground. The NVA (North Vietnamese Army) and the guerilla forces of the Viet Cong used these compounds a lot. When the trap doors leading into these compounds were located, the soldiers who went in to see if the complexes were still occupied were dubbed tunnel rats. They entered armed with L-shaped, Army issue flashlights and a .45-caliber automatic pistol. Since the enemy were small people (relative to Americans) they built their tunnels to accommodate their own needs. Therefore, tunnel rats were usually slim—the only ones who could fit into narrow tunnels and close quarters.

This is a story about a modern-day tunnel rat who went way above and beyond the call of duty to catch a killer. That officer's name was Steve Murdock. Why did he go above and beyond? Because he got really pissed off.

My partner, Frank Scoggins, and I were called into the duty lieutenant's office one day and his exact words to us were, "You two have a capital murder scene I think you can at least partially clear. Your victim was shot and killed in a possible carjacking and patrol has one suspect in custody and another on the ground. Head toward McCarty and the

610 Loop. Happy trails, guys."

We arrived on the scene in about thirty minutes and got briefed by some on-scene officers. A crime scene unit was on deck and I started an overview to document the scene. The victim was a mid-thirties white male, lying dead by the side of the freeway service road. His name was John Mason and he had been shot once in the back. According to witnesses, Mason had jumped out of the left rear passenger's door of a car, and the car's driver jumped out and fired two shots at him with a black-colored pistol, sending Mason to the ground. The victim's hands were tied in front of him with a leather belt when we arrived–most likely his own belt.

What was immediately known, according to witnesses interviewed at the scene by the primary officers, was that the Mercury four-door sedan abandoned at the scene had been driven there by a twenty-year-old black male named Delano Brown. Brown was the scholar that was in police custody, and he was singing like the proverbial bird. He also had the dead man's wallet in his left front pocket when he was arrested. The Mercury was registered to the victim, who lived in the Clear Lake area of Houston, a long way from where he was killed. Brown and the man he was naming as his partner in this armed robbery and carjacking lived in the part of town where murder took place. The suspects in the case were street-wise young males that did not work but wore two-hundred-fifty-dollar tennis shoes. They had been in trouble with the law several times and were unlikely to have risen above what they were because they did not want to.

The two crooks had carjacked their victim from a strip center parking lot just as the victim was leaving his dentist's office. After nabbing Mason's car—with Mason inside—

they drove around Houston getting money from ATM machines using their hostage's credit card. A traffic snarl gave Mason the opportunity to try and make his escape. He jumped from the car and ran down the service road's left shoulder, toward the next major intersection. This made Mason's kidnappers mad. As Mason ran, the driver stepped out the car and fired on him. Then the dumbards figured out they were jammed up in traffic and they too had to run off on foot. Attempting their own escape, they ran right past their victim, who was lying on the ground, and made it to the intersection where they broke left and headed under the freeway. The slower of the two suspects was tackled by a construction worker who had seen the victim flee and get shot down. The suspect who was in the lead ran under the freeway and continued on half a block until he came to one of Houston's channelized, concreted bayous. He ducked down into it and ran parallel to the freeway. Uniformed cops hit the area en masse, and police helicopters began an intensive search from the air.

When Frank and I arrived, I had the scene portion to describe and Frank took the witnesses. He began with the witnesses that Patrol had detained and then walked to the bayou area to see if anyone had seen where our suspect went. Frank found an old man seated on his front porch who told him he had seen the one man run half a block down the road from the freeway and then run east down the bayou bank for 100 feet before turning downhill into the fifty-foot-deep concrete covered bank. From his porch the witness could see either side of the bayou bank for at least half a mile. He said the man in question (who was wearing a yellow shirt) did not come up either bayou bank nor did he ever come back into his line of vision. His line of sight began about 200 feet or more from where the suspect turned down the bayou bank. Frank returned to the scene and went over what he had been told with the uniformed officers who were present. Steve Murdock was one of the officers on scene who was involved in the search and he felt certain that the suspect had ducked into one of the large concrete storm drain tunnels that run along the sides of every drainage bayou in Houston. Murdock got his rechargeable flashlight, borrowed a pair of calf high rubber boots, and began searching the storm drains that came into the bayou on the side the suspect was last seen.

On the second or third drain pipe, Murdock spotted tracks in the shallow water leading into the interior of the drainage system. He could also hear the suspect splashing as he walked in the dark through the maze of tunnels. Murdock exited the drain pipe and told Frank that our suspect had gone underground, and that he was going in after him. Murdock would later tell me that Frank's words to him always stuck with him. He said, "Don't get yourself hurt. Now if you have to kill him down there it's gonna be me and Foster that make your shooting. The Internal Affairs guys and the civil rights section won't slog through that muck and you know we'll take care of you."

So Steve Murdock took off on his own, hunting an armed man who fled a robbery/murder scene. After he had gone a few hundred feet the pipes—which began at about four feet in diameter—would neck down to about three feet high for a while, and then open into large chambers where other drainage pipes funneled in from surrounding areas. After a couple of hundred yards Murdock was beneath the eight-lane 610 Loop freeway and both of the two-lane freeway service roads that paralleled it. Murdock was able to follow the tracks the suspect left in the mud on the bottom of the pipes, and hear him splashing on the water as he fled in the dark. From time to time, Murdock would climb a rebar ladder that led to a manhole. These were located above the huge gathering chambers where multiple storm sewer pipes came together. Murdock later told me that there were rats in there as big as house cats and no end of snakes.

When he got to the far side of the freeway, Murdock stuck his handheld radio antenna through one of the holes in a manhole cover and called for units to meet him. The cover was removed and a very muddy Steve Murdock came into the daylight. He said he knew the suspect was close because he could hear him breathing. He needed two men with flashlights to join him and he was going back down after the crook. Murdock also told the volunteers that he was going in first, and that any shooting that was going to occur was going to be done by him. His words were that he did not want to be shot in the back or hit by somebody else's ricochet. The three men went down and illuminated the next chamber. Murdock called out for their suspect to come out with his hands up or they would come in shooting. The laser sight on Murdock's Glock .40-caliber pistol stayed on the suspect's head as he crawled out of a narrow pipe. He was taken into custody and gave a full confession that evening.

Murdock transferred to another north side Houston patrol station a short time after this murder. While on duty his patrol car was hit broadside in the driver's door by a speeding vehicle. Steve was transported to Hermann Hospital by air ambulance. His heart stopped three times during that trip. He was accompanied in the helicopter by an injured child that had been picked up just before his car crash and injury. He survived and returned to duty several months later, where he studied hard and was promoted to the rank of sergeant.

Steve was in contact with John Mason's widow several times over the years. She and John had been trying to start a family for quite a while. On the day he was murdered, she had just called to tell him the good news that their dream of parenthood was coming true. He was headed home when he was robbed and murdered.

Murdock later transferred from patrol into Homicide where he now works on the day shift. His aggressive policing fits well in the Investigations Bureau. He admits his actions in the storm sewers were more than a bit dangerous since the suspect could easily have hidden away and ambushed him. Murdock was astounded that the crook was able to travel as far as he did in complete darkness, and all the while not get bitten by a snake.

Scoggins and I felt that the serpents were simply extending a professional courtesy to the fleeing suspect. Murdock's motivation that day was anger—all the way to the ground. His actions and initiative in that case went way beyond the norm.

Since that day I have referred to Steve Murdock by the title of Tunnel Rat, and for some reason he still speaks to me.

•PREDATORS AMONG US•

When I began writing this book I contacted friends and former co-workers, asking each if they had a career case, or one that they were exposed to that they were impressed with. One of those I contacted was a hard-working investigator named Ismael F. Flores, better known as Iffy Flores. Iffy is a humble man by nature and was both a hard worker and a dogged investigator. I was fortunate enough to be his supervisor for a couple of years. Whenever I had a case come in that really needed working, I would hand it to him and his partner, Jude Vigil, and tell them, "This son of a bitch needs to go to jail" and the rest was history. They were the kind of guys that got things done. They liked paid overtime and the adrenaline rush that comes from sticking a gun in a crook's face and telling him not to move or you'll kill him.

Iffy was a south Texan (Corpus Christi) and Jude hailed from north central New Mexico. I called Iffy one morning and asked if he had a career case he would be willing to share and allow me to write about. He said he did not, but that he had watched John Parker work a case that impressed the heck out of him. He said John would not stop chasing the crook in one particular case, and even worked the case on his own time. I asked him to touch base with John and see if he was interested in talking to me about that case. I wanted to evaluate the story to see if it would fit in this collection. Only when I interviewed John did I learn that Iffy worked the case with John. True to form, Iffy only mentioned John hounding the case until the crook went to prison for a long hitch.

John came into the police department after meeting and marrying his wife. She was an officer and he had been in the funeral home business prior to their marriage. After joining the department, he bounced around a bit and finally found his home in Homicide. Some folks thought it funny a former mortician found his way into dealing with homicides.

Iffy Flores went from the Army to the Texas Department of Corrections and finally onto the police department. He made it to Homicide, which fulfilled his lifelong dream of working as a homicide detective. Iffy and his father had both served their country by joining the Army, and Iffy told me his father, while on his death bed, said to him, "Don't worry son, I'm Army." *Being Army* meant he was tough and could handle facing death. Three generations of Flores men that I know of were Army. I never told Iffy but I could relate to the situation.

This is a story about a vicious killer and a cop who stayed on his case and hunted him down. A bit of luck and a bunch of tenacity goes a long way during investigations. And so it was in the murder of Elmore Johnson and the attempted murder of his younger brother Alex.

These two young black men were both shot during the course of an armed robbery during a parking lot carjacking near the intersection of Fondren and South Gessner roads in Houston. The Johnson brothers were from Victoria, Texas and would drive to Houston—a three-hour drive—four or five days a week to attend barber college. They were in the school's parking lot when they were shot.

The two victims were sitting in their car during a break from classes, listening to the radio and smoking cigarettes. They were seated in a really clean, nine-year-old, light yellow Cadillac. The suspect walked up on the driver's side of the car, pointed a handgun though the open window, and demanded the brothers' money and car keys. Alex Johnson was in the passenger's seat. He grabbed the keys from the ignition, jumped out of the car and took off at a dead run. Elmore jumped out of the car and followed him. Shots were fired. Elmore ran six parking spaces over and collapsed in an empty parking space. He died where he fell. The robber first fired shots through the open driver's window into the car and then ran around to the back of the car where he fired across the trunk of the car at the fleeing Alex Johnson. Alex was struck once in the back and fell to the pavement. The suspect then ran over to where Alex lay and picked up the car keys from beside the young man. The shooter returned to the Cadillac, backed it up and pulled out onto Fondren Road.

Only one person at the scene claimed to have witnessed the whole event, from the time of hearing the first gunshot to seeing Elmore and Alex both fall to the ground, and the suspect driving off in the victims' car. The sole witness was a black male named Cleatus Prejean from Oakdale, Louisiana. Prejean was in town visiting a girlfriend from back home and he'd stopped by the barber college to get a cheap haircut. Prejean claimed he had seen a young, dark-skinned black male of medium height and weight walk up to the yellow Cadillac and jerk the driver's side door open. According to Prejean, the suspect pulled a man out from behind the wheel and fired a shot into his frontal chest or stomach area. He said the car's front passenger jumped out and ran back toward the school and that he was shot by the suspect as he ran away. Prejean said Alex lay there as the shooter jogged up and picked up what looked like a ring of keys and ran back to the car and drove off in it. No one got the license plate number of the car as it left the lot. There was some broken safety glass six parking places east of the spot the dead body lay, but Prejean was positive of the facts as he related them and said the glass had nothing to do with the murder scene.

Iffy and John both felt something was not quite right with the scene, but took the witness's information at face value. The dead man lay in the middle of the parking space and the cars on the passengers and driver's sides both were dirty and showed no places anyone may have brushed up against them in a struggle or while attempting to flee the gunman.

The family of the victims was contacted and they were able to supply investigators with the car's license plate number. It was logged into the computer as taken in a capital murder and put out in a general broadcast. Although the scene did not quite pan out, the cops had to play with the cards that were dealt them.

Alex Johnson was in surgery for two hours and, due to the necessity of a breathing tube, could not be interviewed for at least twenty-four hours. After the scene description was noted, photos and measurements taken, the detectives went to the morgue, filed an autopsy request on Elmore Johnson, and charted his wounds for a diagram. Following that, the news release was posted and the preliminary offense report was entered.

Then next evening at 5:30 p.m., John Parker received a call from the Allen Parish, Louisiana, Sheriff's Department. Allen Parish is located in the southwest part of Louisiana, near the Texas border. While the best known city in the parish is Kinder, home of the Coushatta Casino, the town of Oakdale—population 7,700—also lies in Allen Parish. The sheriff's department told Parker that an unknown female called their non-emergency number advising them of the location of a Cadillac taken in a robbery-homicide in Houston. She also named Melvin Broussard as the killer and the man who drove the car into Oakdale, but abandoned it just outside the city limits.

The Allen Parish Sheriff's Department said they had the car under surveillance and asked if John wanted them to continue to watch it or tow it in. John asked them to continue to watch it for a few hours before towing it in for processing. After a few hours of surveillance, there was no activity, so the car was towed in. The county mounties in Louisiana did not have a print stall so the car was towed to a garage where they secured it. As it turned out, the sheriff's department also had twenty-eight-year old Melvin Broussard in their system, with a record of violent crimes, and mug shots and fingerprints were available for the asking.

John checked with his duty lieutenant and was advised a day shift crime scene unit was to be sent to Oakdale the following morning but that John was not authorized to go along. John and Iffy were scheduled off the following two days, so John called home about nine that night and asked his wife if she'd like to join him for a drive to Louisiana the next day. Iffy had family plans etched in stone for the next day, so Mr. and Mrs. Parker made the run to watch the car being processed and get the photo and fingerprints on a possible suspect named Melvin Broussard.

Upon arriving in Oakdale, John first observed the interior of the front passenger's side door. He saw bullet strikes on the outside edge of the driver's door and to the post between the front and rear doors. The strikes were high enough that they would have traveled and struck a car parked next to the passenger's side of the car. This caused John to think of, and wonder about, the broken glass six spaces over from the parking place where Elmore Johnson died. It also struck John as odd that their only witness, their possible suspect, and the stolen and abandoned vehicle now all had connections to the small town of Oakdale, Louisiana. As a rule cops don't believe in coincidence.

The stolen car's interior yielded some items of value. Investigators found pieces of paper from a Krispy Kreme Donut shop, a burger place, and a Western Union location—all situated between Houston and Louisiana. A check of security cameras at the drive-up window of the donut shop produced a good video showing the car and its license plate, but not the car's occupants or driver.

The Western Union location, however, had video of a man picking up money, although images were not clear. That video may have been good for elimination purposes but very little else. The Western Union money order connected to the receipt found in the car, however, showed to have been sent by Latrice Everett of Houston, living at 11911 Fondren Rd., Apartment 1125. All of the pieces of paper recovered from the car were taken to the Houston Police Department fingerprint lab where they were fumed, and Melvin Broussard's thumbprint was detected on one edge of one of the documents.

A probable cause arrest warrant (also called a pocket warrant) was obtained from the Harris County District Attorney's Office for Melvin Broussard. This warrant allowed police to arrest and hold the suspect, and put him in a lineup for the purpose of attempting to identify him as a murder suspect. John and Iffy headed straight to Latrice Everett's apartment. A car was found in her parking space that had brand new plates on it. It was obvious the plates were new because that was the only thing clean about the car. But the plates were indeed registered to Ms. Everett and that car. When the detectives knocked at the door Latrice answered and was shocked. She said that yes, Melvin was a friend of hers and that he had recently visited for a few days, but he left about a week prior. She denied any knowledge of any robbery or murder. She said Melvin left with some friend of his (claiming not to know his friend's name) and went home to Louisiana.

She admitted wiring money to Melvin after he called and said they needed thirty dollars for gasoline to get home on. She claimed ignorance of the situation, but her eyes and body language said otherwise. Unfortunately the strip shopping center where the robbery-homicide took place had no security cameras set up that might have recorded the whole incident, or shown Latrice Everett's car present. Latrice said she did not have a valid phone number on Melvin any longer. He'd had a disposable phone she used to call, she said, but she'd tried to call it a few times over the previous week and got a recording that the number was no longer in service. The investigators somehow forgot to mention that they had an arrest warrant for Missing in Action Melvin.

The detectives put together a group of photos in a folder that included a shot of Melvin Broussard. They showed it to Alex Johnson, the dead man's brother, and Cleatus Prejean, the only witness to the murder they could find. Prejean looked at the photos and picked out a fill-in photo, saying "He kinda looks like that." Alex Johnson immediately made a positive identification of Melvin Broussard. Alex's comment upon making the positive identification was unusual. He said that there was no doubt in his mind that was his brother's killer and he said he would know that face in Hell. Cleatus Prejean moved out of his girlfriend's apartment and disappeared.

Alex Johnson told investigators that when the robbery went down he grabbed the keys and jumped from the car and the shots were being fired as he exited the car. He said his brother Elmore was right behind him when he came out of the car. Alex broke right, running toward the rear of the car and Elmore ran to the front of the car and then broke right. Alex said he was running back toward the barber school when he was shot in the back and fell to the pavement.

The next action the detectives took was to file a full-blown charge of capital murder. This would assist in extradition from Louisiana to Texas, if need be. The Allen Parish Sheriff's Department was contacted repeatedly asking their help in locating and arresting the murder suspect Melvin Broussard. For some reason the Louisiana cops never could (or never would) get around to hunting for the wanted suspect from their jurisdiction. It was later determined that a relative of the suspect's was a local law enforcement officer and was running interference for the wanted man. This is way outside the norm, because Louisiana policemen have always been known to go out of their way to help a fellow officer, anytime they can. The only place I've ever known of that did otherwise was the Shreveport (Louisiana) police, who, in my experience, were collectively about as worthless as a hope chest in a cat house. (Discussing this with other investigators, it appears Shreveport PD has been consistent in their behavior for a long time.)

After meeting Latrice Everett for the first time, John Parker tried to keep tabs on the girlfriend of their prime suspect. Soon after their interview, however, Latrice left her apartment and did not return for three weeks. She was a single mom who may have feared for her child, or for her own freedom. Whatever the cause, something obviously was bothering her. In the course of beating the bushes for the crook, investigators came up with another Houston transplant from Oakdale, Louisiana, and another former girlfriend of Broussard. He just showed up one day at her apartment unannounced after they'd visited back and forth several times on the telephone. He wanted a place to stay. Melvin explained to her that he would be in Houston for a week on that occasion and he said he was there to do some "Licks", meaning armed robberies. When he asked her if she knew of any potential targets with money he could rob, she balked. Due to her reaction he moved on.

The murder investigation continued, but all the while John and Iffy kept getting more murder cases dropped on them, along with assisting other detectives with other cases. John always found time to come back to the Johnson murder case and it was obvious that he was not ever going to let up on his hunt for Broussard.

One evening after supper, John and Iffy were driving back to the office and Parker said, "Let's go drop in on Latrice and see if she's heard any more from good old Melvin." So they drove to Latrice's apartment. She answered their knock at the door, obviously quite nervous, and she said she did not know where Melvin was, nor had she heard from him. From a positon standing at the front door, the detectives could see back into the apartment's master bedroom. On one side of the door leading into the back bedroom, John saw part of one arm. The detectives entered the apartment and arrested Melvin and handcuffed him. They sat him on the floor with his back up against a wall.

Melvin was a lean and muscular twenty-eight-year old,

and immediately began squirming and attempting to slide up the wall into a standing position. The cops knew they had a potential runner on their hands so they dragged him out onto the floor and put him face down, even putting a chair atop him so he would have to knock it over if he attempted to get up. It was a busy night for patrol so the detectives had to wait forty-five minutes to get a uniformed unit to transport their suspect. Their suspect was very agitated and hostile, but Iffy tried to keep Melvin occupied by talking with him and asking him questions. Patrol finally arrived and transported their prisoner.

Iffy and John transported Latrice to the Homicide Division to interview her. She was slow to talk at first, adopting the old hear no evil, see no evil, and speak no evil routine. John went to the interview room where Melvin was detained and Iffy kept after Latrice. After a while, Iffy got Latrice crying and the truth came out. Melvin is a violent guy and she is afraid he might harm her, or her child.

Latrice told Iffy that Melvin follows a routine when he comes to Houston. He rides the bus from Coushatta Casino there in Kinder, Louisiana, to Houston for fifteen dollars and he gets someone to pick him up. He pulls several armed robberies and then buys drugs and returns to Louisiana in a stolen car. Latrice had been with him the day he carjacked the Johnson brothers. She said he was ready to return to Louisiana and asked her to drive him around so he could spot a car to drive home in. They were on South Gessner near Fondren and he pointed to a parking lot and told her pull into it. He directed her to pull up behind a yellow Cadillac. She did as he asked, he got out of the car and she drove off as he walked up to the driver's side of the Cadillac. She did not see or hear what followed. Latrice said Melvin traveled with a backpack and he kept his pistol in a white bag or pouch inside it. She told Iffy that when Melvin got out of her car that day he had the white pouch in his hand. She said his choice in the way of a weapon was a .380 automatic pistol.

While Iffy was with Latrice, John was trying to get Broussard to confess to the killing. The closest thing to an admission of guilt was an outburst from their highly animated suspect. Broussard was told about the recovery of the Cadillac and his fingerprints found inside it. At that, Broussard exclaimed, "Fuck the law in Oakdale! Fuck the law in Louisiana! I rob people—I shoot at people—but I don't kill people." John became tired of dealing with the idiot killer and put him in jail.

When Iffy and John took their witness, Latrice Everett, home they had her point out the location she dropped Broussard on the day of the murder. It was six parking places away from where Elmore Johnson dropped to the pavement, mortally wounded. The site of the shooting was the spot where the safety glass had been found. John's gut feeling had been correct; the witness from Broussard's home town had lied to them. The detectives took their witness back to her apartment and she showed them the suspect's backpack. It contained nothing incriminating.

What was of interest, though, were two telephone recordings that had been left by Melvin Broussard for his girlfriend Latrice. They both said the same thing: "Babe, stick with the story—they don't have a thing." Broussard had left the messages by using the telephone in the AFIS room at the jail. AFIS stands for Automatic Fingerprint Identification System. It is a computerized fingerprint system that verifies identifications and catches people with criminal histories trying to use assumed names. AFIS had also caught suspects from crime scene fingerprints. Those individuals were not in the system before, but the crime scene prints linked them to the crime when they were arrested on unrelated matters.

Broussard sat in jail for a year and a half before his case went to trial. He was ultimately sentenced to forty years in the Texas prison system. He was (and I am sure still is) mad-dog mean. When the day comes that he is released, he will continue to be a threat to decent people. His homeboy, Cleatus Prejean, never was located even if the court had wanted to use him as a witness.

Iffy Flores is an interesting character in his own right. He was a hard-working cop who carried a full-sized Model 92 Beretta .40-caliber pistol, in a holster that he had built into one of his cowboy boots. He has always treated all people decently and was creative in his policing practices. One scoundrel he arrested was a bit of an escape artist so Iffy handcuffed him to the spare tire of his car. He kept the prisoner chained up like that throughout the whole booking process—all the way into the jail. That crook complained long and loud about first having to ride to the police station cuffed to a tire and rim, and then carrying a spare tire around with him throughout the police station. Iffy tried to keep suspects off balance to keep their minds off mischief. It seemed to work to his benefit.

On another occasion a drunken, low-rent suspect hit a child with his car, killing the child. After killing the little girl the idiot stepped out of his car to view his handiwork, and laughed about what he'd done. He then got back into his car and drove off. Iffy started beating the bushes and put the word out that he was out to kill the idiot. Iffy came on quite strong when telling the suspect's friends and family how badly he wanted to put Stupid in the ground. The suspect heard about Iffy's threats and demeanor and turned himself in. Not only did the worthless wad of living matter show up at the police station, but he gave a full confession. His motive was to save himself from "that crazy policeman." Stupid figured jail was the only place he would be safe from the wrath of Iffy Flores.

This robbery/homicide case was something that happens with many investigators from time to time. There was something about this investigation that John Parker took personally. That is why he clawed and even spent his own time and money working this case. This behavior is not uncommon, and often the motivation of the investigator is not clear to the rest of the world, or maybe even himself. Welcome to a side of police work you will rarely, if ever, hear about.

•PHIL•

Philip Boykin was an Army combat veteran—like his father and grandfather before him had been. He stood two inches above six feet tall in his stocking feet and looked leaner than he actually was. His dark hair was slightly curly and fell a bit over his ears. With a heart-shaped face, the man looked like Michelangelo's statue of David if you dressed it in dark-colored jeans, a snap-tab shirt and western boots. To say women had an interest in the man would be an understatement. Phil may well have been too damned good looking for his own good.

In the mid-1970s, police departments in America were full of former military types. Drafted at nineteen made you twenty-one at mustering-out time. If you had not been smoking too much stuff from Uncle Ho Chi Min's victory garden then you were what police departments were looking for. You were capable of working in a regimented organization and had learned how to work both within and around rules and regulations.

Phil captured the immediate interest of women everywhere, but any relationship he had with a woman was usually short-term. He once said many only lasted long enough for there to be three short strokes and a cry of joy. I think that his thousand-yard stare was sort of mysterious, and maybe the shrapnel scars on his chest and back made him even more rugged looking. He was quiet, and at times prone to reflection and fitful sleep. He often went for long, late night walks alone. I don't know if it was the bird-with-a-broken-wing group, or those women who wanted to mother him that hung around.

The side of Phil that his coworkers saw was that he was absolutely fearless and never rattled, or even prone to act in an excited manner. However, due to his actions one night, he also set police departmental policy forever.

Police department policies about minor things like grooming standards, or how to wear a uniform properly, are written by bean counter types. The policies set out regarding high-speed chases, or undercover operations such as drug buys, come about usually following a royal shit storm, some public relations nightmare, or a lawsuit that screams of negligence. Phil initiated the current policy regarding undercover drug buys, or what is called a buy-bust situation.

When Phil went forth to run warrants or fight bad guys he carried two nickel-plated .45-caliber Colt Government Model pistols. Both guns had good quality sights added to them and sported honest-to-God elephant ivory grips, and ambidextrous thumb safeties. Both weapons were carried in the middle of his back with the butt of either gun facing out to either side. This put the pistol grips about the level of his kidneys. Yes, the man was a bit of a dandy, but he would have been able to buy dope from his own mother had she been dealing.

Phil had sent up a half-ounce heroin buy in a barrio sector of less-than-scenic southeast Houston. His informant had fallen for a one gram case and that conviction would make him a three-time loser. Habitual criminal status would have gotten him a mandatory life sentence. The problem was that Phil's partner was off that night, so our boy went off to do the deal alone. This sort of action is now called Tombstone Courage in survival training courses. Now, you should know that there are two kinds of people inside the dope arena. There are those that sell drugs and those that claim to sell drugs but commit armed robberies instead. Few people ripped off in drug transactions call the police or file complaints with the Better Business Bureau.

The scholar Phil met with that night decided to play the armed robbery angle. The deal went down with both players seated in the front of Phil's two-door undercover car. Phil had his flash roll of cash and his test kit to check the dope's purity, and Stupid came equipped with a bag of power and a handgun. The crook handed over his bag of powder and pulled his gun. Phil leaned forward and put his chest against the car's steering wheel. With his left hand he grabbed the gun butt of the weapon located over his left kidney, and from behind his back he fired four rounds.

The illicit pharmaceutical vendor was very much DRT (dead right there), as the saying goes. Then Phil got on the police radio mounted under the driver's seat of his car and calmly called it in.

605 to Narcotics Base.

600 to 605: Go ahead.

605 to 600: Be advised I'm in a parking lot inbound on the Gulf Freeway and south Wayside. I will need a supervisor, a Homicide Unit, and a white body car for one male.

600 to 605: You advise you have just been involved in a shooting?

605: That is clear.

600 to 605: Will you need an ambulance at your location?

605: That is negative—there is really no need to send one out.

Policy changed within forty-eight hours regarding backup, and having a location known to the Narcotics desk who would, in turn, advise the watch command just prior to execution of said warrant or arrest.

Phil worked SWAT prior to his assignment of multiple years in Narcotics. He finally transferred to Criminal Intelligence and then worked Cargo Theft prior to his retirement. He always held that the uniformed patrolman had the most dangerous job and should be getting hazardous duty pay.

Phil went through five or six marriages during his years on the police department. About a year after he retired he contracted Parkinson's disease. His last wife (who was about twenty years his junior) had him served with divorce papers one morning while he sat at the kitchen table drinking coffee. His beloved left the house for work just ten minutes before the constable knocked at the door.

About an hour after getting served with the civil papers, Phil called the city of Pearland's police dispatcher and reported a shooting had just taken place in his backyard. He then went outside and unlocked the backyard gate so the responding cops could get in. He sat down in a lawn chair and put a 200-grain CCI brand hollow-cavity bullet through his brain. He always favored those bullets which had been called "Flying Ashtrays" back in the day.

Many that knew Phil, in hindsight agreed that he may well have been regularly putting himself in positions where someone might have been able to kill him. He never had, however, given the crooks the edge. Had they gotten him, they would have had to earn it.

Suicide by one's own firearm was for many years called "The Policeman's Disease." Phil was always a pleasant enough and a stand-up kind of guy who had brass balls that clanged when he walked. Neither bravado nor swaggering around was his style. I, for one, always thought he was a good guy.

I hope he took his demons with him. They had it coming. I don't think he really deserved it, though.

•SANTERIA MURDER•

Santeria, like Voodoo, is a pagan religion of sorts that has its roots in Africa. It stemmed from the slaves brought into Cuba, and what are now other island Caribbean nations that the Spanish once colonized. Santeria now exists here in the United States and is regularly run up on by cops. The religion, which is similar to Catholicism in belief and practice, includes animal—and sometimes human—sacrifice which supposedly gives power and protection to those who practice it. Mexican Christians sometimes have personal altars in their homes but do not include the Santeria worshiper's cauldron with the animal bones or skulls, antlers, iron railroad spikes or large nails.

Police work is, at times, like being a licensed Peeping Tom, but often you see and hear more than you ever really wanted or needed to hear. When you speak to people who admit to practicing this sort of religion they will tell you that you can't possible understand it because "You've got to first believe in its power." Some Mexican dope dealers also now favor Santeria worship, with its hedonistic and evil overtones. Innocent people have been kidnapped and sacrificed to supposedly give more power to Santeria practitioners. Cannibalism also crops up among this group–most commonly the eating of someone's heart–to give the practitioners even more power, particularly if the person killed was a rival or enemy. These people are to be classed among the sadistic and truly evil. *Power* or *powerful* are terms they use a lot, and power is what they covet.

This murder investigation began when part of a body was discovered in northwest Houston, Texas. Willie Bunch was a street person who lived a hand-to-mouth existence. He was poking around, looking for something of value on the median that ran between the Northwest Freeway and its service road. As Willie was walking near the freeway's intersection with West 34th Street, he saw a taped-up cardboard box that was about twenty-eight inches square. Ripping off the tape, he found what was determined to be a woman's torso and a left arm. Willie went stark raving, bat guano crazy, and ran completely across the service road (without looking) and about a half block down the street to a gas station, where he had an employee call 911 to report dead body parts. Actually, the store clerk reported a crazy man jumping up and down, babbling about a dead body in a cardboard box. The clerk's parting words with the dispatcher were "Just send somebody down here quick to get this crazy SOB outta my store. He's scaring off all the customers."

A patrol unit made the scene and freaked out as well, but not as badly as Willie Bunch had. The blue suits called the Homicide duty lieutenant. Sergeants Mike Peters and Jim Ramsey got the scene assignment, and for the next week or so they worked double shifts with no days off. The human remains had obviously been dumped in the grassy median, so the scene itself yielded few clues. The box was submitted to the crime lab, as was the powder blue nylon blanket that was wrapped around the body. The female torso and arm were taken to the Harris County Medical Examiner's Office for processing. The fingerprints on the found hand got no local identification and the medical examiner reported that the remains were those of a female in her mid-twenties, possibly Hispanic, who had been in good health and was about two months pregnant. The cause of death was determined to have been manual strangulation. No rope or ligature had been used to strangle or choke the life from the victim's body.

From there, detectives began working missing person reports to try and first identify the body they, and then figure out where she was last seen or heard from. A report taken that same morning listed Elaina Garza, a twenty-four-year-old Hispanic female, as missing from her place of employment at the Fiesta liquor store which was located on the northwest corner of the intersection of Bellaire Boulevard and Hillcroft Avenue. Her work hours were from two in the afternoon until nine at night, and while Elaina had failed to show up for work, her car was in the Fiesta parking lot, still parked where she'd left it on her previous shift. Her coworkers said she was a good person, in a happy marriage, and very happy about expecting her first child, due in about seven months. When asked about any problems with customers or coworkers her boss said that there was a customer who seemed to be somewhat infatuated with Elaina, and he came by almost daily. He might buy a pack of cigarettes or a pack of gum. Elaina was the only person he would ever do business with. Further, it had been noted that the man never came into the store if Elaina was not on duty. The man's name was Geraldo Martinez and it was known that he lived in the apartments at the corner of Bissonnet and Rampart streets because another of the ladies working in the liquor store lived there also. The store manager gave the cops a good description of Elaina's admirer and the car he drove. The admirer was said to look like a troll and was "butt ugly."

Looking at the picture her husband provided, it was obvious Elaina was a pretty young woman with a beautiful smile. A check with the Texas Department of Public Safety positively identified Elaina from her thumbprint taken when she obtained her Texas state driver's license.

Investigators, who already had a pile of phone messages to wade through and paperwork to complete, now needed to research a certain fellow named Geraldo Martinez. He had a criminal record for assault with bodily injury, but nothing really startling or damning. Martinez had been in this country for over a decade after arriving from Cuba as an adult refugee. Sergeant Bill Stevens and D. D. Shirley hooked up with detectives Ramsey and Peters to run down leads, which came in day and night. At least the cops now had fingerprints to compare to whatever turned up on the cardboard box Elaina had been stuffed into. Caught up on their paperwork by about day four, Ramsey and Peters went and knocked on Martinez's front door. The sergeants brought along a crime scene unit just in case they hit pay dirt. Martinez answered the door and the investigators asked if they could come in. He obliged.

The detectives advised him they were investigating the murder of a lady named Elaina Garza who had worked at the Fiesta liquor store. Martinez said he'd read about it in the newspaper and seen the story on television, and that it was such a shame. She seemed to be a nice lady when he'd made purchases at that store before. As they entered the apartment, the cops immediately keyed in on the fact that there was a metal caldron on the coffee table in front of the couch. It contained a couple of railroad spikes, deer antlers, a cigar and some long nails. Ramsey spoke up, saying, "Ah, I see you practice Santeria." Martinez responded with an immediate, "Oh no, I'm good Catholic." The detectives looked around the apartment and noticed a blue nylon comforter on the bed that matched the blanket that had been wrapped around the torso of Elaina Garza. They presented Martinez with a consent to search form which he readily signed, saying he had nothing to hide. Had he refused to sign it, detectives would never have had enough probable cause required to obtain a search warrant.

The dresser in the bedroom was painted the same color as some paint smears that were evident on the blue blanket found in the box with the torso. But the tell-tale piece of evidence that sealed the deal for detectives was when they sprayed the bathtub with luminol. The whole of the drain area, and a few flecks around the edges of the tub glowed a whitish-blue, even with the overhead bathroom light simply turned off. With this, Ramsey told Elaina's admirer, "Guess what, Geraldo? That means a quantity of blood was spilled in your bathtub. Now you are under arrest for the murder of Elaina Garza."

The suspect was transported to the Homicide Division for interrogation. Spanish-speaking Sergeant Cecil Mosqueda and Officer Jaime Escalante were called in to assist in the questioning. Martinez was Cuban born and came to America as an adult, so the investigators did not want him to be able to claim he did not understand his statement (if he made one) and potentially lose it as evidence in court. This was a one-shot deal, so a major piece of evidence was critical.

Geraldo Martinez first said he was not responsible for anyone's murder. However, after a bit, the suspect claimed that he had been forced into this whole situation through association with his *padrina,* or godmother. He said she was an evil person, a *bruja* (witch), and that she forced him into involvement in the murder. Martinez gave investigators her name and luckily, she was listed as a theft complainant in the Houston PD computer system. A Spanish-speaking detective drove out to her house and picked her up, planning to use her in a power play against the suspect. Godmothers are often heavy-hitters in many Hispanic cultures. When they arrive back at Homicide, Martinez was shocked to see his *padrina* walk through the door. After a verbal exchange in their rapid-fire Cuban Spanish, he told her (in Spanish) to hit him. She slapped the dog water out of him, and all the cops present winced. He repeated the request four more times, and each time she obliged by knocking the snot out of him. Then her killer godson hung his head and told the detectives he would tell them the truth about exactly what had happened.

He told them of his great love for Elaina and that he did not take her by force but that she willingly agreed to go with him to his apartment. There he tried to tell her of his feelings and love for her, but she rejected his love. He said she spat on him and in a fit of rage he choked her, but that he never meant to kill her. It had been an accident, he said. After she was dead he had to get the body out of the apartment and he had to dismember her to do so. Martinez said he had to put her body parts in several cardboard boxes in order to carry them off. Yes, the blue blanket was his. He claimed he'd just gotten scared and did not know what else to do. He told the investigators where he dumped the other boxes containing the remaining pieces of Elaina Garza's body.

The night of Martinez's confession, the rest of Elaina's body was recovered from a vacant lot near the intersection of West 34th Street and Longpoint Street. The medical examiner reported that the body parts had been separated at the joints, and the cuts were clean and professional. Detective Peters wondered if Martinez had some professional training because the dismemberment was so well done. Investigators later learned that their suspect had been a butcher while in Cuba.

Martinez was charged with murder and put in jail. As usual, once pay dirt was struck there were other day shift investigators (at their lieutenants' prompting) who wanted to jump into the case. At this point in the case, there was only a bit of mop-up to do, and it took a couple of days to put everything on paper so the case could be understood by someone who had not been there from day one.

This was a high-pressure case characterized by long hours and bad coffee. The case began on a Friday and ended on a Friday. The stress was enough that Mike Peters reported losing ten pounds in a week's time. It is one of those experiences people will tell you they are better persons for having lived through, but really don't care to repeat ever again. Putting a twisted animal in a cage was a good thing. It does not, however, counterbalance the murder of a pleasant young lady and her unborn child. The other victim in this case was Elaina's husband, who reportedly was a decent, hard-working young man. The actions of Geraldo Martinez will forever mark the lives of the other surviving family members and loved ones left behind as well. They too become victims of one of the many predators that walk the face of this earth.

Detectives Stevens and Shirley figured out that the boxes used to secret the dead woman's remains from Martinez's apartment had been obtained from behind a furniture store near where he lived.

Geraldo demanded a jury trial. The case took less than

a week to try, and a jury found him guilty and sentenced him to life in prison. At the time of this writing, he is still incarcerated and hopefully will die in a cage so that he can't hurt another innocent person.

An interesting aside in this case is that there had been a psychics' convention in Houston the week of this investigation. That produced no end of leads, none of which would pan out. One of these soothsayers even came down to Homicide put their two bits in. Their motive in doing so was, most likely, to be able to put in their resume they had assisted in a murder investigation with Houston Homicide detectives.

Ours is an interesting world, particularly if viewed from afar.

•CHUCKLES•

Dedicated to the memory of a man who never faced a fate worse than sobriety.

Chuckles was a fifty-five-year-old white male street person. He hung out regularly in the skid row, or Mission District, of Fort Worth, Texas. He was wheelchair bound and the source of a multitude of police calls for service. On top of that, Chuckles was a royal pain in the ass to deal with. He was never known to assault an officer, but when arrested he would whine and cry, as well as scream and carry on as if he were being skinned alive. If he'd been drinking and you arrested him, he was not above pissing in the back seat of your patrol car. Even if he was cuffed behind his back, he would piss in his pants in order to get even with you. Needless to say, he was not a favorite with the law enforcement community.

He was on social security disability and would panhandle in the downtown area around hotels and restaurants from time to time. For him, a good line that produced cash regularly was, "Hey Buddy could you help a disabled veteran?" On a good day this gentleman smelled like a wet dog, or if it is possible, maybe even worse. I guess you could say he was the sort of fellow only a mother could love being around, and then only if she carried a can of Lysol with her. Like most street people, he carried a knife and had used it in the past on some street vermin who had tried to rob him. Stupid he wasn't, and he would keep his hands out in front of him when dealing with cops. If they told him they were going to arrest him, he would politely tell them where his knife was as they were putting on their latex gloves to search him. That was about the only time he was polite when dealing with police officers, however.

Chuckles hung around the downtown area for a number of years. When told to move on or threatened with jail, he began claiming that he was tired of being messed with by the Fort Worth cops and if he had the funds he would go back to his hometown of Waco, Texas. In Waco, he said, the cops were nice and the winters not as harsh. One enterprising young officer named Reilly, who'd gotten tired of dealing with "Hell on Wheels" decided to take Chuckles up on his claim. He asked Chuckles one day if he was serious about leaving, and if Fort Worth PD paid for his bus ticket, would he really move back to Waco. On his wino word of honor, the mayor of Lancaster Avenue said he would indeed relocate if FWPD provided the means for him to do so. Reilly drove directly to the bus station and found out the price of a one-way ticket to Waco. The wheels of change were put in motion.

A one-gallon jar with a coin slot cut in its top was placed in the central station roll call room, with a sign affixed reading, "Bus Ticket Fund to Relocate Chuckles to Waco." From pocket change alone, the fundraising goal was reached in a week and Chuckles was good to his word. A lift gate van was procured (and later fumigated), and himself was transported to the bus station. Reilly's sergeant put him on special assignment that day to make sure Chuckles got on the bus and stayed on it until it pulled away from the station. It was a good day for the troops in Cowtown when the Greyhound bus hauled "El Funko" south and beyond the city limits. They marveled at how something as simple as some pocket change could help clean up a town.

Almost exactly two months following the day of his departure from Fort Worth, Chuckles reappeared. The only thing about him that changed was that his wheelchair now sported Waco Police Department stickers all over the back of it. They too had pooled their pocket change and sent a problem child packing. Chuckles said that his old hometown had changed too much and he really didn't like it there anymore. Besides, the cops were no longer friendly and the residents there were now too cheap to give money to panhandlers. Fort Worth was now his home and he was ever so glad to be back.

The best laid plans of men can often go astray. The tragedy of the return of Chuckles turned into one of the better urban legends, even if sadly it was true for the men and women of Fort Worth who had to deal with him. However, it seems he may have picked up a new trick while he was on sabbatical to Waco. By the time Chuckles returned to Fort Worth, he had added to his wino street theatre repertoire. Post-Waco, when the cops went to put the Habeas Grabass upon Chuckles, he would throw himself to the pavement or sidewalk and scream out to passersby, "Help! Help! They're beating me. Take pictures, please. They're gonna murder me if they get a chance."

Trust me–you could not make this stuff up, even if you were smoking an opium pipe.

•THE VOODOO QUEEN•

Edward James Jones was a highly effeminate, thirty-year-old black male cab driver in Houston, Texas. He was born in Kentucky and claimed to have two years of college education. For a time he lived in New Orleans and worked the tourist trade as a Tarot card reader. Five years before he came to Houston by way of Louisiana, Jones was charged with robbery in the state of Florida. He was determined to be not guilty by reason of insanity in the robbery case. In their infinite wisdom, the powers that be put Jones back on the streets and enrolled him in a Miami-based, outpatient mental health clinic for treatment. The Houston detectives who eventually dealt with Eddie Jones dubbed him "Sweet Eddie Sue." In reality, there was nothing sweet about Edward Jones. He was both dangerous and compulsive, and could change gears and explode at any moment.

The Houston case began as an armed robbery and shooting at an insurance agency. It became capital murder when the resident agent died from a gunshot wound.

The killing took place inside an office building near the Astrodome complex, several blocks east of the intersection of South Main and the 610 Loop. The agency where the crime occurred specialized in selling policies to low-income minorities. The clients (generally blacks and Asians) might be paid weekly, biweekly, or monthly. The agent running this agency had a staff which included both black and Asian men that sold and serviced small insurance policies, mostly commonly life or burial. Servicing accounts meant each individual agent had a list of clients that he or she would manage, and part of that duty was knowing how and when their clients would be paid so they could collect payments, which typically took place in person. What's more, these low-income insurance companies typically collect their fees in cash, which means these agents and agencies are at times targeted by predators in the 'hood.

In this case, the suspect kicked things off by walking up to the pay window at the agency. The pay window was located inside the business' lobby area, which was accessed from a solid door off the third floor hallway. The agency was configured much like a doctor's office, with a receptionist sitting behind a sliding glass window in the lobby area, across from the main entrance. The receptionist answered the phone and took insurance payments as well. On the day of the robbery, the armed man entered, wearing a nylon stocking over his face, and pointed a blued-steel revolver at the woman behind the window. When she saw the gun she screamed, jumped up, and ran and hid behind some filing cabinets. The resident agent, George Rojas, walked to the reception area to see what all the commotion was about. The armed man pointed his gun at Rojas and demanded, "Give me the money Mister Big." Rojas complied and did as he was told. He put the cash and checks in a plastic sack from the trash can beside the intake desk and handed it all to the robber. Rojas told the armed man to "Please calm down and take the money. Nobody needs to get hurt." Rojas took a step back, at which time the suspect ordered him back to the window and demanded the Rolex watch Rojas wore on his left wrist. George Rojas responded, "Sure—take it. Just please don't hurt anyone." The suspect then extended his gun hand straight out and fired twice at Rojas, striking him one time in the chest.

The suspect's bullet was fired from an inexpensive five-shot .38 caliber revolver made by Rohm (pronounced Rome) and bore the model number 31. Its trigger pull was harsh (exceeding twelve pounds, and gritty), enough that it could explain the downward angle the bullet traveled. To fire that weapon double-action (like a cap gun), you really had to pull pretty hard, or jerk the trigger. Rojas suffered a through-and-through bullet wound that entered his left chest five and a half inches below the top of his left shoulder and exited his right back, nine inches below the top of his shoulder. Entry and exit wounds were about ten inches apart and on either side of the midline of the body. The bullet effectively coursed downward through his heart and ended his life. The distance determination test (burned powder particles) done on the dead man's shirt later showed the gun was fired from a distance at least two or more feet away from the victim. That bullet was collected from inside a sheetrock wall. The second bullet hit no living person but hit a metal file cabinet and went through the file drawer and into the wall behind it. Both projectiles were recovered.

Upon firing his revolver the robber, Edward James Jones ran from the office with the money bag in one hand and his pistol in the other. He was followed by one of the agency's male employees, down the staircase and onto the street. Another businessman who was walking up to the building's front entry door joined in the chase as it moved outside. Then a group of construction workers from an apartment complex down the street fell in, chasing after the suspect as well. Jones turned as he ran and fired several shots toward the citizens chasing him. Once Jones started shooting, some of the men stopped chasing him, while others continued after him. One of the posse members described the scene as resembling a horseback chase in one of the old Roy Rogers movies, where the bad guy turns in his saddle and fires back at the approaching good guys. The bad guy in this case stumbled while running through a vacant lot one block down the street. He was then tackled by the co-worker of the late George Rojas. The rest of the posse joined in and held the misunderstood mother's son until the police arrived.

Though Jones drove a Yellow Cab, he was not a company employee but rented the cab on a daily or weekly basis from the company. He had, in fact, parked his cab on a side street on the far side of the vacant lot he was running through when he stumbled and was pounced upon by a group of folks who were not afraid to get involved.

Detectives Scott "Doby" Dobyanski and Bobby Williams were assigned this case. They split up the investigation so one investigator described the physical scene and the other detailed witness statements and interviews. Crime Scene Officer Ron Horowitz made the scene too. He diagramed and photographed the scene, collecting and submitted all evidence he could find.

The scene detectives had the suspect transported to the Homicide Division to see if someone could get a confession from him. The suspect's story was that he had stopped his cab on a side street just off South Main and had stepped outside of it when he was jumped by a group of men. They held him for the police and said he had robbed someone. Jones claimed no knowledge of any robbery or shooting.

The first day of a murder investigation is spent getting the information about victims, witnesses, and a scene description. It will often take a full day to get the basics from witnesses and send them to the station for sworn, notarized statements. Before the witnesses arrive at your office you'd best call the duty lieutenant and tell him the basic facts of the case, whether you have witnesses you are sending down, and any suspect information you have.

Any suspect arrested at the scene has to be taken to the Homicide office and interviewed. You may opt to have him run past a municipal court judge for a legal warning. If a suspect decides to talk, it's nice to have a copy of the legal warning in hand–official documentation that the judge has advised the dirt bag of his rights and the dirt bag acknowledged understanding his rights. After that, you hope he will be stupid enough to give someone a confession. If he does, you have to get it down on paper as a witnessed and signed statement, or recorded on video or audio. Then, in your spare time you run by the morgue to file an autopsy request and do a wound chart of the body.

The day after this particular murder, during their follow-up investigation, Williams and Doby found out there had recently been a notable firing at the insurance agency, a man that may be of interest. They were told there had been hard feelings between the murder victim, Rojas, and David Dubois, the individual he'd fired the week before. When that former employee's information was obtained, investigators were surprised to learn that Dubois and the arrested suspect, Jones, shared the same home address. The detectives were told that after being fired, Dubois told Rojas on his way out the door, "I'll get even with you for this." Investigators later learned Dubois was not only Edward Jones' roommate, but also his lover. Dubois was arrested on some outstanding traffic warrants and taken to Homicide for questioning. He admitted being Jones' roommate but denied any involvement in the robbery. Jones was interviewed while housed in the county jail and he too denied Dubois was involved at all. However, after Dubois entered the picture, Jones changed his story and told investigators he stopped by the office building to use the restroom. In this version of his story, Jones said that upon entering the building he was accosted by an armed man who chased after him, shooting all the while. Williams and Doby asked their suspect about the single knee-high stocking and its wrapper that they found on the front seat of his locked cab. It was the same color and length as the one they found discarded in the stairway the shooter fled down. Jones claimed no knowledge of how it got in his cab and accused the cops of planting evidence and trying to frame him for a murder he did not commit.

Jones claimed total innocence in the robbery/homicide he was now charged with. He now also denied his earlier story about just having stepped out of his cab when he was jumped by a group of men. The two detectives kept digging but could never link the roommate David Dubois to the death or robbery.

Jury selection in capital murder trials in Texas is a long and drawn-out process which often goes on for weeks. Each potential juror is questioned individually by both the defense and prosecution. They are asked a series of questions about knowing the defendant, any policemen, if they have ever been a victim of a crime, and if they could be unbiased in determining guilt or innocence. During jury selection, Jones decided he'd had enough fun and broke and ran from the courtroom. He made it down three flights of stairs and ran a couple of blocks from the courthouse before being recaptured.

Rather than continuing to run, Jones had chosen to

jump into the front passenger seat of a nondescript, four-door passenger car occupied by a lone woman sitting in the driver's seat. It turned out the woman in the car was an FBI agent named Ann Myers. Ann was well versed in close quarter combat (having taught it for two years at the FBI Academy in Quantico, Virginia). She was also left-handed. As soon as Eddie Jones jumped into her car he blurted out, "Get out of here fast bitch, or I'll kill you too." Ann's right hand came off the steering wheel and Jones got a pair of tremendous elbow strikes to the left side of his head. Ann grabbed him by the throat and put her duty pistol in his face. Scared she was not–really pissed off she truly was.

Jones was taken back into custody though he wobbled a bit as he walked back to the courthouse and claimed he needed medical treatment for a bad case of double vision. The court bailiff who chased after Jones told the judge that it was obvious the lady FBI agent had made quite an impression on the defendant. He described the blows that Jones took to his head were such that they made it snap back and forth like a paddleball toy in action.

Thereafter, whenever Edward Jones came out of a holding cell he wore an unusual shackle throughout the court proceedings. It looked like a ten-inch-long piece of thin-walled pipe that was hinged on the back side. It fit over his knee area on one leg and was locked on the front with a key lock. With the shackle in place, he was forced to walk around with one leg completely straight, unable to bend that knee at all. This kept him from being able to run, or even walk very fast. His gait was said to be that of the man who played the role of Chester on the old TV series *Gunsmoke*.

Before the defendant attempted his escape from custody he had been sitting at the defense table with his two court-appointed attorneys. Both attorneys had once been prosecutors with the district attorney's office in Houston. Jones was allowed a legal pad and a sharpened Number Two pencil to make notes which he would to pass to his attorneys. At one point during the trial, he disagreed with something one of his attorneys told him so Eddie James threatened to stab that lawyer in the eye with his pencil. After that exchange Eddie's school supplies were taken away from him.

Author's note: I guess if he'd been forced to use a crayon during the rest of the trial it would have caused jurors to speculate as to the defendant's mental state and thereby might have been prejudicial to the defense. The jury might have equated it to Hannibal Lecter's restriction to felt-tipped pens, for much the same reason – though even a felt-tipped pen might cause some damage if properly applied to an eyeball.

The jury had no problem finding Edward Jones guilty of capital murder and sentenced him to death by lethal injection. There is a mandatory appeal program in Texas, mandated by law in all capital murder convictions. Jones's first appeal was filed, regarding his mental competence to stand trial. It appears that good old Eddie Jim had been charged in Florida with robbery five years before he became a murderer in Texas. Florida contended, though, that he should be found not guilty by reason of insanity and for some reason put him in an outpatient mental health program.

Due to the prior Florida insanity verdict, the State of Texas had Jones tested by two psychiatrists before his trial and then again after the first appeal was filed. As the appeals process ground on slowly Jones decided he was tired of prison and wanted to stop the appeals process and get on with his execution. Each doctor that examined Jones found him to be sane and said that he understood the charges against him. They also found he was not suicidal regarding his desire to stop his appeals. In other words, he was sane enough to kill.

There was a last-minute attempt to stop the execution where Jones' mother testified before the Fifth Circuit Court of Appeals. She said her son had been a kind and loving child until he began practicing black magic, Voodoo, and witchcraft. She also said that he'd claimed to have participated in six ritualistic killings before his arrest. He further supposedly made the claim to her that the corpse of a year-old child was thrown off a bridge into a river after it had been beheaded during a sacrifice made to some Voodoo god.

Death row inmates are allowed to order a last meal of their choice prior to their execution. Jones requested rhaeakunda dirt, a substance used in Voodoo rituals. It is supposed to consist of graveyard dirt and is looked upon by the practitioners of Voodoo as a very powerful substance. They reportedly use it in the casting of spells against other people, for safeguarding one's self and in the making of love potions. The most powerful rhaeakunda dirt is supposed to be that which is obtained it from atop the grave of a close friend.

Jones said he wished to use the dirt to somehow mark his body (he did not elaborate just how), whereby his spirit could pass on to another realm and not become a ghost. Grave dirt is reportedly the power mainstay of people calling themselves Hoodoos. Jones warned the prison staff that if he were not able to ingest the rhaekunda dirt that his ghost would fly around and haunt the town of Huntsville, Texas for a period of three hundred years. His request for the dirt was denied, so his second choice regarding his last earthly meal was vanilla yogurt.

Before the execution was carried out Jones was asked if he had any final words. He did. His last words on this earth were, "I myself did not kill anyone, but I go to my death without begging for my life. I will not humiliate myself. I will let no man break me." He then smiled and winked at the observers on the other side of a glass window and said the words, "Hare Krishna." After Jones finished his statement the cocktail of lethal drugs was injected into his saline drip and he was executed. During his intake session at the diagnostic prison unit in Huntsville, Texas, Jones said that at different times in his life he had been both a follower of the Hare Krishna religious sect and also a Voodoo priest.

Neither of the homicide detectives who worked this case chose to view the execution. In their opinions, "Sweet Eddie Sue" (as they called him) was not worth the time or the effort to drive seventy-five miles one way just to see him off. In the early morning hours one June 26th, between midnight and daybreak, a newly-surprised face arrived in Hell.

The only point of interest in this case (as far as I am concerned) was that four members of the Texas Supreme Court ruled that they believed there existed a degree of doubt about Jones's mental competency regarding his ability to stop the appeals process and get on with his execution. However, it takes five members of that court to stop an execution, and there were not that many interested in prolonging the life of this misguided mother's son. Therefore Jones' mental state was cleared by their review and there was not enough horsepower in that ruling to stop the State of Texas from killing him. Thereby justice was served and another violent criminal was permanently rehabilitated.

An interesting aside:

This was a death penalty case. All convicted capital murderers can potentially receive the death penalty upon conviction. However, a prosecutor must actively seek the death penalty. Now the other options are life in prison or life without the possibility of parole. At the time of this trial, the choices were either life or death. The main consideration in giving the death penalty is that the jury must believe that the convicted murderer, if ever paroled, would be an ongoing threat to society. In reality, a life sentence typically only equates to twenty calendar years served.

There are so many capital murders cases filed in Harris County, Texas that the Harris County District Attorney's Office reviews them in blocks of seven cases and picks out the worst crime in that lot to prosecute as a death penalty case. The cost to the county taxpayers from the time of arrest for capital murder, through the trial and appeals process upon their conviction, then finally administering the death penalty is well over a million dollars. There is simply not enough money to kill them all. Now that the sentence of life without the possibility of parole has become a possible sentence in capital cases, the number of Houston of slugs sentenced to die has dropped off. Prior to the life-without-parole sentence, convicted persons either got a life sentence (which means twenty to twenty-five years) or death by lethal injection.

In capital murder cases in Florida the courts often pick a jury in the morning and start the trial that same day after lunch. The percentages of guilty verdicts in Texas and of those in Florida are reportedly pretty much the same. The court-appointed attorneys in Florida, however, make a whole lot less money on their court-appointed cases. You see, in Texas these attorneys get paid for their courtroom time, much like a meter in a cab left running. The longer the meter runs the more cash the attorney pockets. Texas' legislature is full of criminal defense attorneys, so this cash cow program is not about to change.

Another point of interest is that some individuals who are wrapped up in the study of the paranormal (ghosts) claim Edward Jones' spirit does in fact fly above Huntsville, Texas, haunting the town to this day.

•THE CAPITAL MURDERERS•

Freddy Gomez was a good, decent, hard-working kid. Everybody who knew him told you so. He worked all one summer doing construction and used his earnings to buy a five-year-old, super clean Honda sedan. I met him just before his senior year of high school was to begin. We met because he was shot to death on the basketball court of a school near his family's home.

At the time of Freddy's death, Frank Scoggins and I were partners up in Homicide. Freddy had been shooting baskets with a neighbor kid who was going into the ninth grade at J. Frank Doby high school–the same school Freddy attended. The subdivision where Freddy grew up, and where he ultimately died, was called Skyscraper Shadows. It is located in southeast Houston, not too far from Hobby Airport. Long before Freddy was born, developers had visions of a boom in that area of the city, imagining it filled with nice homes and safe neighborhoods. That never came to pass.

The only known witness (other than the suspects) to Freddy's murder was Larry Hammond, the neighbor kid Freddy was shooting hoops with.

My partner, Frank Scoggins, was the son of a San Antonio used car salesman and a hard-working cop. He'd done two hitches in the Army and was a darned fine investigator. Scoggins never met a stranger and drove like a bat out of Hell. He had the gift of gab and watching him deal with a crook, you would think he was closing the sale on a used car. He'd been through Army sniper training and viewed work as something you did to support your fishing and hunting programs. Scoggins was a great shot with rifles, pistols and shotguns. My wife often said, "While you are working with Frank, I don't worry about where you two go or how many doors you kick. Just don't let Frank drive." Now back to the case.

While shooting baskets, Freddy Gomez and Larry Hammond were approached by a pair of unknown young black males who walked up on foot. These two males were both described as being eighteen to twenty years old, each about six feet tall and wearing billed caps. Only one of the two males did any talking. He first said to Freddy, "Man that sure is a clean car" while pointing at the Honda Freddy had just bought. He then asked, "Do y'all know whose it is?" Freddy said it was his and the talker pulled out a black-colored revolver from behind his back. His next comment was, "You can give me the keys then" as he smiled, showing off a gold front tooth. Freddy shook his head and told him, "No, you need to go to work and go buy one of your own." That's when Gold Tooth eared back the hammer on his revolver and pointed it at Freddy's face. Freddy threw the basketball at the robber and was shot in the face. His injury was a through-and-through wound that coursed from front to back. (According to the medical examiner, death was instantaneous. I hope so, for the kid's sake.) After shooting Freddy, the two males took off running, without the car or its keys. All they took was a young man's life.

Our only witness, Larry Hammond, ran across the

street and beat on the door of a house, telling the man who answered the door about the shooting and pleading with him to call an ambulance. Larry was a good witness and co-operated fully. Larry's father was present when we arrived and encouraged him to tell us everything he could think of. His dad looked like he had a rough life but had risen above it to raise his family in a middle-class working neighborhood. The kid gave a sworn statement detailing the events of the murder.

Departmental sketch artist Lois Gibson came in and made a composite drawing of the killer based on Larry's description. Lois commented on how good the young man was to work with. Larry's dad was visibly shaken, realizing how close his son had been to a needless killing. The reality of how cheap life is to lower forms of life is a harsh concept to deal with, particularly when it strikes close to home. Larry's dad made the comment, "Nobody should ever have to bury a child of theirs. We will cooperate in any way we can. I'm not worried about anybody coming around trying to cause us trouble. If they come by, I'll call you to come pick up what's left of them."

The story of Freddy's murder was on the news, television, radio and the newspaper. The composite picture appeared in the paper and on TV. No calls came in. Scoggins made up posters with the composite picture and the dead kid's picture as well. He stuck them up in convenience stores and at Freddy's school. No calls came in. One afternoon, a month after the murder, Larry Hammond called Frank and said, "I saw the guy that killed my friend. He's a student at Doby High School and I'm told his name is Jacoby Wilks."

I'd taken a few days off, and my partner Scoggins came in early the next day with another sergeant named Alfred Herrmann. Herrmann was a stone-faced and droll old-timer with about twenty-five more years on the department than Frank Scoggins. They went to the high school and waited in the vice principal's office while Jacoby Wilks was pulled out of class. Herrmann was normally not impressed by much, but when the potential suspect walked in, Herrmann said, "Damn, I think there's a picture of you hanging on the wall down in our offices." Wilks was an eighteen-year-old, in his junior year there at school. He'd had a few brushes with the law already but nothing major. He was cooperative with the two investigators, but contended he knew nothing about the murder, and though the composite picture did look somewhat like him, it was not him.

Wilks was transported to the southeast command station and questioned further. He claimed to know nothing about Freddy's death. Scoggins asked Wilks if he wanted to take a polygraph exam to prove his innocence, and he said he did. Scoggins set up the exam and left Wilks for about ten to fifteen minutes with two experienced investigators named Todd Miller and John Swaim. When Scoggins returned, Miller and Swaim told him they thought he had the wrong man, and that Wilks had not done it. The polygraph examiner hooked the possible suspect up to the machine and ran the test questions. Then he went over a group of questions regarding the murder in question. Then he called Scoggins. Wilks was unhooked from the machine and the examiner said, "He did it. The only things he answered truthfully were the test questions and his name." At that, Wilks blurted out, "All right, I did it but I'm not gonna tell you who was with me." Scoggins did not care, because they had the shooter. Scoggins took Wilks' confession and put him in jail. Charges were filed that night.

The news the next evening featured a television reporter named Jerome Grey interviewing the aunt of Jacoby Wilks.

The aunt was his legal guardian because Wilks' mother had been "mistakenly" sent to prison. Auntie contended Wilks was innocent, and that furthermore, the police had picked up her nephew from school, taken him to the police station, and beaten him until he signed a confession. Frank Scoggins was pissed, to say the very least. He called the reporter, Jerome Grey, and asked why he had not contacted him directly about the allegations.

Scoggins told Grey that homicide investigators were damned proud of how they took care of business, and their word had to be good. To have it dragged around on the six o'clock news without a chance to rebut it was pretty darned rotten, and unprofessional on the part of the reporter. Grey apologized and Frank demanded an on-air retraction. That retraction never came.

After Jacoby Wilks was charged, the vice principal of Doby High School called, saying he had something to pass along in the matter. He said he had not wanted to skew the investigation, but that he had stopped Jacoby a few weeks earlier and told him to stop wearing a cap in school, which was a violation of their policy. According to the vice principal, the cap bore the words *Capital Murderers*. Wilks told him it was the name of a rap group. It appears the murder may well have been a gang initiation that turned fatal for Freddy Gomez. As part of their induction, prospective gang members are often required to commit a felony. Freddy Gomez was most likely the price for Jacoby Wilks' gang membership.

When this case came together it did so in a hurry. There were no clues until the one eyewitness came through like gangbusters. This was a career case for Frank Scoggins because of the victim. Most murder victims are not true innocents, but Freddy Gomez was. The reasons behind this murder are incomprehensible to normal people. Normal people can't think like street vermin. Freddy was a good kid, and a good student who deserved more out of life. It was not a case that brought a commendation from the chief of police, or recognition from Scoggins' peers. It was personal.

Sometimes investigators take cases personally. Just why you take a specific case to heart is hard to say. You see baby killings and abuse of old people, but it's critical to approach them at an objective, professional level or you can wind up in prison yourself. Cops don't do well in prison.

During this investigation, Scoggins went by the malls in southeast Houston and asked around at T-shirt and cap shops, finally locating one that had made a half dozen caps with *Capital Murderers* stitched across their fronts. The shop owner said he now had a policy in effect that banned the printing of any slogan even remotely gang-related. He wanted none of the thugs' business.

As this case went on, it got even more interesting. The defense attorney for Jacoby Wilks produced a witness who claimed to have seen the entire thing go down, and reportedly was ready to testify that not only was Jacoby Wilks not the shooter, but that the shooter did not even come close to looking like Wilks. Scoggins and the chief prosecutor, Debbie Mantooth, went and picked up the new witness to interview him. The three of them sat down in an interview room at the southeast command station and began to talk about the crime. The witness, Marvis Chambers, began by saying he saw the whole situation unfold, with two black guys walking up to the Hispanic and his black friend shooting baskets. He then he saw the one pull out a gun and shoot the Hispanic kid. The two blacks ran away and the younger black kid ran to a house across the street. Scoggins started asking questions. Was the shooter right- or left-handed? What kind of gun did he have? Was it black in color, or silver? Which direction did the two guys run? Do you know that if you knowingly give false testimony in a court hearing you can be charged with aggravated perjury? It is a felony and there is no probation for that charge–if convicted, you have to serve felony jail time. Chambers suddenly backed away from his statement and finally admitted he had been in his backyard when he heard the single shot that was fired. Chambers admitted that the attorney for Jacoby Wilks had told him what to say, and that the lawyer also knew Chambers had actually never witnessed anything pertaining to this matter.

Jacoby Wilks was sentenced to some serious hard time.

•THE TEXAS STATE HOTEL•

Houston, Texas in the dead of winter can be as cold and dismal as sin. With its high humidity the cold wind goes right through you. Mix cold and damp with overcast and gloomy—with no greenery—and you have the setting for the murder of Ralph Thomas Mapp.

Ralph was a forty-nine-year-old disabled veteran. He lived at the Texas State Hotel in the drab concrete canyons of downtown Houston. He got by on his military disability pension, and from time to time he had to sell his pain medications to get through to the end of the month. The first of every month he paid one month's rent to the hotel and bought a meal ticket so he had two meals a day. He walked with a cane due to a debilitating back injury that his pain meds only took the edge off of. The Veterans Administration hospital never gave him enough dope to be completely free of pain.

The Texas State Hotel was once the spot where a lot of movers and shakers in Houston met to cut deals, scheme, and plan both state and national political moves. Back in its heyday, the street level housed several restaurants, gift shops, and both a barber shop and beauty salon. By the time Ralph Mapp took up residence there it was seedy and sliding toward skid row. In fact, many of the working poor and lower economic crowd were moving *out* of it because living there was becoming just too rough and dangerous. Ralph lived there for only a couple of months before he was robbed and murdered. This hotel was a place that could have been described as being just outside the very gates of Hell—maybe two hundred feet from the edge of the pit. Some people succeeded in escaping this zone before it consumed them. This sector of Houston knew no boundaries regarding lifestyles, colors or creeds. Further, it is populated by all age groups. And everyone within this combat zone world knows one thing for certain: Evil beings moved about freely as they lived and hunted.

At the time Ralph lived at the hotel, Teresa Lynd ran the restaurant. When Ralph had missed two days' worth of meals, Teresa asked D. J. Kelly, the front desk manager, if Ralph was out of town, or in the hospital or something. D. J. and Ralph were friendly and D. J. too thought it odd he had neither seen nor spoken to Ralph in a couple of days. D. J. called room 1125 and when he got no answer he went upstairs and used his pass key to enter Ralph's room. He found the naked and very dead remains of Ralph Mapp on the floor near the foot of his bed, and there was what looked like blood smears on a couple of walls. After taking a look around D. J. stepped into the hall, closed the door and went downstairs to call the police.

Bobby "Cuz" Williams and Scott "Doby" Dobyanski (working the afternoon three in the afternoon to eleven at night shift) were in southwest Houston trying to run down a lead in an old case when they were bumped on their detective channel police radio. The duty lieutenant directed them to make the murder scene at the Texas State Hotel. They arrived in about thirty minutes and were met by an investigator from the medical examiner's office and a transport body car. At the scene, in Ralph's room, there was plenty of disorder and it was obvious a fight had taken place. It likely started in the area of the bathroom and went into the main part of the room. The room was a basic hotel room with a bathroom, and a single bedroom, and one closet. There were blood drips on the floor of the bathroom and visible blood smears on the door frame of the bathroom as well. More blood drops were on the floor leading to the area where the body was found, and another smear on both the wall near the foot of the bed and the bedclothes. It appeared the room had been searched and a pair of pants was found on the floor outside the bathroom with its pockets turned inside out. The victim's wallet was on the floor with its contents scattered as if someone had gone through it looking for cash. Dresser drawers were pulled out and the contents obviously been gone through or dumped on the floor. There were a couple of empty pill bottles with the dead man's name on them—one a narcotic pain killer and the other for a super strong Tylenol. Both scripts were from the Veteran's Administration Hospital pharmacy in Houston.

A crime scene unit with Officer Ken Hilleman aboard was dispatched to take photographs, diagram the scene, dust for fingerprints, and collect any evidence the detectives wanted. Hilleman was a happy-go-lucky guy who had been raised around a mom and pop funeral home in St. Louis, Missouri. In his childhood home bodies were embalmed in the basement, the parlor was on the first floor and the family lived upstairs. So dealing with the dead was kind of second nature to him. Hilleman pointed out that the single window in the room—which faced out onto the street—was open when officers arrived, therefore with the cold air streaming in, establishing a time of death would be sketchy.

Hilleman was almost obsessive-compulsive about any

hobby he took up, be it photography, skeet shooting or scuba diving. The joke around Homicide was that Hilleman did nothing in moderation, and his wife was hoping he never developed a serious interest in sex. At the scene, Hilleman took blood samples from multiple different sites throughout the room, in case the suspect or suspects might have been cut also. Suspects regularly cut themselves accidentally (usually on the hands) when stabbing other folks.

The body car personnel were allowed to roll the body over (after the photos and measurements) to load it onto a gurney and transport it to the morgue for autopsy. When discovered, the body had been face down on the floor. And when Ralph Mapp was rolled over it was obvious he died with an erection. He had a prosthetic penis pump and was ready for action when killed. With this discovery, the two detectives, the body car men, and the medical examiner's investigator all gave the dead man a round of applause. Then the jokes started. "He died with his boots on" and "You can't keep a good man down" were a couple of the quips. After a few minutes the novelty wore off and the body was loaded and rolled out to the waiting van. It is hard to explain that gallows humor keeps people in a carnage-filled world from internalizing what they see and keeps them somehow better grounded and sane. It's not something you talk about in Sunday school class.

After notes were made to carefully document the scene the detectives went to the morgue to view the body. They examined wounds and catalogued them for a chart that would go in the case file. As part of their process, they also filed an autopsy request, which included a request for fingernail scrapings—in case the dead man had scratched or clawed some skin off his attacker before he was stabbed to death. Detectives noted a couple of cuts on the victim's hands indicating he was trying to fend off the attack, and two stab wounds to the body. The cuts to his hands are called defensive wounds, meaning they were inflicted while he was attempting to either ward off or defend himself from his knife-wielding killer.

Ralph was also wearing a condom, so given that detail—and the fact that he was naked—indicated there may be a male or female sex partner involved, possibly a prostitute. Homicide investigators learn to not discount any possibilities. Male homosexual prostitutes regularly kill their tricks, and knives are often the weapon of choice, for some reason. Every detective makes one or two of these murder scenes a year, on average.

Williams and Doby discussed the matter and decided not to include in their report that the dead man had a penis pump activated. They did not want a disabled combat vet to be the butt of a bunch of courthouse jokes. Therefore, that detail never appeared in the body of the report.

The next day they called the morgue and talked with Dr. Vladimir Paurongoa (known to all as Dr. V. P.) about the particulars of the murder. Dr. V. P. told them the victim had been strangled with something narrow, like a cord, but that the cause of death was a stab wound to the heart. The other stab wound was in the victim's liver but it likely would not have been fatal unless their victim got a secondary infection from the county hospital system. Not long after their visit with the medical examiner, they received a phone call from Sergeant Bill Brown in Vice who said he had a paid informant who lived in the Texas State Hotel and that his informant knew who had killed their complainant, and why. Brown set up a meeting between the homicide investigators and his informant for seven o'clock that evening at the Vice office.

When Williams and Doby met with Brown that evening they learned his informant was none other than D. J. Kelly, the front desk manager at the hotel. Kelly and the victim got along and both were US Army veterans. Kelly said Ralph Mapp was a reclusive man who generally stayed in his room. He was also believed to be heterosexual and admitted that he treated himself to a prostitute a couple of times a month if he had the extra money. Mapp drank alcohol but did not regularly frequent bars. Kelly said that in fact this killing involved a hooker-based robbery which led to Ralph's death. Kelly also knew the prostitute involved. She was a youngster named Brandy who had lived in the same hotel up until two days before.

The working girl was supposed to be turning a trick with Ralph, and two guys named John Turner and Don Broyles came in the room to rob him and wound up killing him. Brandy was supposed to be trying to leave town that very night. Kelly said that Turner and Broyles were also said to be talking about leaving town for parts unknown pretty darn soon.

Kelly went on to say his own wife was supposed to be taking Brandy and her two-year-old child to one of the downtown bus stations that very evening so she could return home to Little Rock, Arkansas. Kelly's wife got along with Brandy pretty well and felt sorry for her. His wife had also babysat the two-year-old Tiana several times and was quite taken with the child. Kelly warned them John Turner, the smaller of the two killers, was the one to watch, saying Turner was, "Nothing short but mean and there was something just evil about him." The six-and-a-half-foot tall Don Broyles was allegedly no prize either, but just a follower type for Turner to use. Kelly said he would try and get in touch with his wife and find out if she had taken Brandy to the bus station yet, and if so, which station. He tried to call her before he walked into the Vice office but her phone kept rolling over to her voicemail.

This case was about to kick into overdrive. This is the point where an investigator will call home and tell their spouse they will be home at daybreak, if they're lucky. This was really not unusual for the evening shift, because with a total of twenty investigators split between two squads, this shift makes almost sixty percent of the murders in Houston. The knife and gun club gets most active between nine at night and three in the morning.

Kelly said he was headed back to the hotel, and he now had the both of the Homicide guys' cell phone numbers should something develop.

It took a while for Kelly to catch up with his wife. As soon as he did he called the detectives and said his wife's phone battery had died. She said she'd already left Brandy at the Greyhound bus station. Brandy had run into some guy from her hometown and they were just going to sit around the bus station and visit for a couple of hours until her bus arrived. Williams and Doby went to pick up Kelly and take him with them to the station to point out Brandy.

They had no sooner gotten to their car when Kelly's wife called him back and said Brandy had called her, saying her bus was delayed two more hours but that her hometown family friend had offered to drive her and her child back home to Arkansas in the morning. Brandy and company were supposed to be staying the night in the La Branch Hotel in the downtown area.

The only problem was, there was no La Branch hotel in Houston. The detectives dropped Kelly back off at the hotel and were halfway back to the Homicide office when Kelly called and said his wife was mistaken—the hotel where

Brandy was staying was the Montague Hotel in the downtown area. Another white-knuckled trip (for the passenger), with Williams driving, had them sliding up in front of an honest-to-God flop house. When the two cops walked up to the front desk, all the patrons in the lobby just sort of drifted away. The desk clerk said, "Can I help you officers?" without them even speaking or showing him a badge. When they asked about Brandy, the clerk knew who they were talking about and directed them to a room on the fourth floor.

The door was answered by a green-toothed, twenty-two-year-old hillbilly named Dewayne Crowder, who badly needed a shave and haircut. Upon seeing a badge he said, "Y'all come on in." They identified themselves to Brandy and said they wanted to talk with her about the murder of Ralph Mapp at the Texas State Hotel. She said she knew what they were talking about and said she would be truthful about the whole matter because it was really bothering her. She agreed to go with the detectives to the Homicide office.

Brandy's child was left with Dewayne Crowder but a short time later Kelly's wife took custody of the child and contacted Brandy's family back in Arkansas. The baby's birth father was headed south and expected to be in Houston about eight the next morning. As soon as Williams and Doby got into Homicide, Kelly was calling. He said the two killers were at the restaurant there at the hotel and they'd told him they were going to leave town that night after supper. Kelly said he would try and stall the suspects but the detectives needed to hurry. The two men would be in the hotel restaurant.

Doby and Williams asked the duty lieutenant to assign a detective named Doug Osterberg to take Brandy's confession. Then Lieutenant Beck called for a two-man patrol unit to assist in the arrest of the male suspects. Now, Osterberg was a very capable investigator. He stood six foot four inches tall, and was called Big Bird by his co-workers (after the Sesame Street character). Bird was also a bit of a sanctimonious sort who wore his religion on his sleeve at times. He was not above berating someone for looking at a *Playboy* magazine.

Brandy, the prostitute, was not the sharpest knife in the drawer but she knew how to put her best assets forward. She had very pale skin and straight, blonde hair. Her skin was almost opaque to the point she resembled an albino. Her leading asset, which she blatantly flaunted, was her massive bosom, which she displayed unashamedly, and with abandon. She was wearing a heavy coat when she walked into Homicide.

She was led into a side office by Sergeant Osterberg and upon entering, took off her coat. She was dressed in a low-cut halter top which exposed a large tattoo of a red dragon on the left side of her chest. What's more, her nipples were playing peekaboo with Osterberg the whole time he was interviewing her. She had plenty of information regarding this crime and Osterberg wound up taking a very detailed, four-page statement from her. He would later confess to Dobyanski that the interview and statement took so long because he could not keep his eyes off that tattoo. Brandy's statement was highly detailed and covered much of the robbery planning as well as details about what she saw and heard leading up to the murder. Doby would later confess (but not to Osterberg) that he and Bobby Williams both would have had problems keeping their focus had either of them taken Brandy's statement, for obvious reasons.

While Osterberg was collecting Brandy's statement,

Williams and Doby pulled up in front of the Texas State Hotel at the same time as the marked two-man patrol unit. They went straight into the restaurant and found Kelly seated at the table with two men who both wore dark rimmed eyeglasses. Williams and Doby identified themselves as police and told both men to turn around and put their hands on the wall. The suspects were both handcuffed and searched. Both men carried buck type folding, single-blade knives in sheaths on their belts. Don Broyles also had a three-bladed pocket knife in his right front pants pocket. Doby took custody of all three knives and marked them as to which crook had what before he submitted them to the crime lab the next day. The first order of business was to get these two crooks processed and put in jail.

The two male suspects were separated and transported to Homicide by two different marked units. Don Broyles would give Bobby Williams a full confession while John Turner told Doby he knew nothing of any murder and did not wish to talk to the cops any further. He was taken to the Identification Division where investigators learned he was actually an ex-convict named David Lee Kesterson. Kesterson had no open warrants and did not show to be a wanted or a possible suspect under either his true name, or any of his multiple aliases.

Synopsis of the Confession of Judy Gonzling, aka "Brandy"

Judy Gonzling said she had come to Houston from California to see her boyfriend as they had been discussing marriage. After she'd been in town only a couple of days he decided he wanted out of the relationship and simply left. She had been living in the Texas State Hotel for a couple of weeks trying to get ready to move on with her life. While living there she met Kesterson and Turner, men she knew only as Don and John. On the day of the murder she, Don and John went to a nearby bar called the Golden Stein and drank a few beers. John told her he wanted her to meet an older guy who had lots of money. If she would come along with him, he would give her some cash. Brandy said she did not want to turn a trick with some guy and John told her the old guy would probably only want to talk with her and maybe kiss on her. She reluctantly agreed. John (Kesterson) went to another table where an older guy sat and brought him over to the table and introduced him to Brandy. The old guy introduced himself as R. T. and bought her a beer. They talked for a few minutes and he asked her if she would like to join him in his room. She told him she would be there in thirty minutes. R. T. left and John told her to not mess up the deal because the old guy had Dilaudid and they could sell them for thirty bucks apiece. John told her to have the old guy pay her in Dilaudids. Then, as they were crossing the street to the hotel he changed the plan. He told her to tell the old guy that he needed to take a shower before she would bed him down. Then as soon as R. T. got into the shower she was to open the hotel room door and Don and John would come in and get the guy's dope and money.

What in fact happened when she let the two into the room was that Don and John took up positions on either side of the bathroom door. John had some kind of strap or extension cord between his hands. The old guy opened the bathroom door and said, "Ready or not here I come" as he stepped into the room, completely naked. John came up behind R. T. just as he walked out of the bathroom. He slipped the cord across the old guy's throat and pulled back on him, choking him.

Brandy blurted out, "What is going on?" and Don told her to shut up. John demanded of R. T. "Where's your Dilaudid?" and the old guy said, "I only have two left." John called him a liar and Brandy went to leave. Don told her to go to his room and wait on them. John then told her, "You had better do as you're told or we will kill you too." She did as she was told and went to Don's room. That room was directly below the old guy's room and she related that she heard some banging around on the floor above her. In just a matter of a few minutes John and Don came into their room and John was covered in blood. He was wearing a white thermal shirt and blue jeans. Don did not have any blood on him, however.

Confession of Don Broyles taken by Bobby Williams

Broyles told Williams that he and John Turner (he did not know Kesterson's real name) had been at a bar when they saw a girl named Brandy pick up a guy who also lived there at the Texas State Hotel. They hatched a plan with her to tell the guy to take a shower before she would turn a trick with him. Then she was to let him and John into the room and they were going to steal the old guy's dope. He said the old guy came out of the shower and got into a struggle with the both of them, and they each stabbed the guy one time in the chest. He said they took the guy's money and two Dilaudid pills. Broyles said that the man he knew as John Turner had blood all over the clothes he wore. He said that after the killing they met Brandy down at his room and gave her $70 and she left. He and Turner went to his own room and John took off his bloody shirt and pants and threw them out his tenth floor window and took a shower.

The old guy they'd killed had a stash of 250 more dollars and a couple of ounces of weed taped underneath one of the drawers in his bureau. They split that money and dope down the middle. The cash they gave to Brandy came from the guy's wallet. They got a cab to the area of the North Freeway (I-45) and Crosstimbers and went to a Mexican restaurant. There, they met a guy called Yolo and sold him the Dilaudids and the two bags of weed. John threw the empty Dilaudid bottle over a chain link fence behind that restaurant. Broyles said there was a drainage ditch that ran parallel to and behind the parking lot fence.

After Brandy and Broyles gave their statement, all the suspects were put in the city jail and the detectives got home sometime after three in the morning. Doby, Williams and Big Bird met back at the Homicide office the next day at noon to tie up loose ends and file charges. Their first task was to file charges, and further evidence needed collecting and tagging. Copies were made of the confessions and reports to date, along with the charge paperwork for the district attorney's office. Williams was designated to take the charge information to the intake section of the DA's office and swear to the charges as the affiant.

Doby and Osterberg headed back to the Texas State Hotel to attempt to recover the bloody clothes that Broyles said Kesterson had thrown out of the window of his tenth floor hotel room. When they arrived, the detectives first met with D. J. Kelly, and told him about the bloody clothing they need to search for. Kelly pointed out that there was a solid awning encircling the building on three sides. Kesterson's room had two windows and they both faced out toward Fannin Street. He noted the solid awning provided shade and kept rain off people on the sidewalks but also caught most all of the trash thrown out of the windows by his classy hotel patrons. He suggested they start by looking out the windows on the second floor on the Fannin Street side. It was that easy. Clearly visible was a pair of blue jeans and a white, pullover, long sleeve shirt.

The distance from the window ledge to the top of the awning was approximately four feet. This proved no problem for the six-foot-four Osterberg who climbed out of the window and recovered the evidence.

As Big Bird and Doby were leaving the hotel, Kelly reminded Doby that he was a paid informant, not someone who worked for the police out of the goodness of his heart. Doby assured Kelly he would be rewarded for his assistance, and the two investigators headed back to Homicide to submit their evidence.

The recovered articles of clothing were wet from a recent rain so the detectives took them straight to the Homicide Division's drying room where the clothes were hung to air dry before being submitted to the crime lab for testing. If left wet and put into an evidence bag (required for submission to the lab), mold or viruses would develop, making any identification impossible. Both items of clothing looked like they had blood stains, but only a certified chemist could prove what it really was.

After the drying room, their next stop was the city jail. All three suspects were still there and would be transferred to the county jail that afternoon. The detectives went to the third floor of the jail and pulled Don Broyles out for a few minutes. The blue jeans that the detectives put in the drying room were Wrangler brand, size 34 x 31. They asked the tall, skinny Broyles what his pants size was and he said 31 x 38.

Upon leaving the jail, the detectives headed up the North Freeway to Crosstimbers Street and located the Mexican restaurant Broyles had described. After a ten-minute search in misting rain, the pill bottle with the victim's name was found in the dead grass along the drainage bayou just beyond the parking lot fence. It too was photographed and collected as evidence.

On their way back to Homicide, the detectives made a call to Crime Stoppers of Harris County in an attempt to pay D. J. Kelly for his information that led to the arrest and charging of three capital murder suspects. To the cops' disgust - and later, the anger of D. J. Kelly - all that Crime Stoppers would pay was three hundred and fifty dollars (rewards can be up to $5,000).

Crime Stoppers said the lower than normal amount was due to the information having been submitted after the fact and because Kelly had not contacted them first, which was their usual procedure in these things. The investigators also felt that in the future Kelly would no longer deal with the police, because in his world he was really sticking his neck out. The cops knew that a mercenary individual is loyal as long as you pay him, and don't mistreat or lie to him. They will even give you the names of other cops as references, to vouch for how their dropping a dime on other crooks has worked out in the past.

Many informants would like to be cops, and get a rush out of their association with law enforcement. Mess your snitches over, though, and they will just walk away from you. The ones who are in it for the mon¬ey are the best, as they have a singular goal and will take the calculated risks necessary to achieve it. Their motivations will vary—some want to be friends and hang out with cops. Others seem to like being put on the edge of trouble or risk getting killed if their association with law enforcement was found out. In all honesty they may not know the real reason them¬selves.

When test results came back on the knives submitted to the lab only one tested positive for human blood traces. It was ever so slight and not enough to do anything else with. There were traces of soap found inside the handles of the lock blade knives, which indicated the suspects had tried to cover themselves but either were lazy or did not know they needed to use chlorine bleach to kill off blood residue evidence. Now it was time for supplements to be made—evidence submitted—because the district attorney's office now owned the game. In situations such as these, with three defendants, it becomes time to play let's make a deal. Broyles had a bunch of misdemeanor arrests and one auto theft case. Brandy had never been arrested according to national computer checks. Kesterson (aka John Turner) had a couple of auto thefts and burglaries, and one other homicide arrest before this one. He had spent three years in prison for one auto theft and a burglary.

A grand jury indicted Kesterson for capital murder but Harris County opted not to seek the death penalty. Their decision worked out in the end. Don Broyles and Brandy both agreed to testify for the state in exchange for lesser charges and sentences. Broyles was told the state would not ask for more than thirty years upon his plea to a murder charge. Brandy was to get a ten-year sentence upon a plea of guilty to a burglary charge. In Texas, you need to have more than just co-conspirator testimony to convict someone. In this case, they had knives—one with blood trace evidence—along with clothing soaked in the dead man's blood, and some other evidence to boot.

Kesterson got a court-appointed attorney named Joe Cannon. Cannon was a dapper, older man who presented himself as a southern gentleman attorney. He had a thin, quarter-inch-thick mustache that ran across the top of his upper lip, and wore seersucker suits in the summer time, accessorized with a straw Panama hat. Cannon was pleasant enough to witnesses, and competent enough that he covered the necessary bases so cases were not overturned behind some defense error. He also did not drag out trials forever, and as such was appointed to some heavy duty cases that did not clog up the trial dockets with long-winded motions and such.

The one thing about Joe Cannon, however, that may have jeopardized his clients was his wig. He always wore high-quality suits, but his wig looked like it had been made out of a white string mop—at least in my opinion. Furthermore, the wig never stuck down very well onto his bald head. Particularly during the final argument phase of a jury trial, it was unlikely the jury ever heard a word he was saying. All the jury panel (and everybody else for that matter) was focused on as Joe strutted back and forth, pontificating, was his wig. If you witnessed this scene—watching that string mop sliding around on his head—you feared it was going to slip off and hit the floor at any moment. This is, of course, pure supposition on the part of this author because that was my point of reference, but one backed up by many other detectives who sat through final arguments of this and other trials. Although jury members were looking intently at the defense counsel the whole time, we were sure they were really waiting for that wig to fall off his head.

As a general rule, Joe Cannon did not badger witnesses or the cops. His clients were known to get a whole lot of hard time and even death penalties. To date there has not been a case ever retried due to unintentional distraction of a jury panel. This case was unusual because it is the only time in anyone's memory that Joe Cannon ever gave an investigator a bad time on the witness stand. That investigator turned out to be none other than Doug Osterberg. To cap it off, Osterberg really hated to testify at trials, and it seemed like hours that Cannon was trying to trip him up over his collection of evidence, and procedurally how the clothing was submitted to the crime lab. The whole scene was reminiscent of the O. J. Simpson trial but on a lesser scale—at least as far as Doug was concerned. Everybody else involved got a pass from Lawyer Joe.

It was to no avail though, as Kesterson (aka John Turner) was handed a life sentence, both literally and figuratively. After the trail was over and Kesterson was sentenced, the detectives were leaving the courtroom via the back offices of the court. There, handcuffed to a wooden church pew, was Kesterson's partner in crime, the scrawny and long-haired Don Broyles. He was waiting to enter his guilty plea in exchange for only thirty years in prison. Beside him on the bench was a Bible. He told Doby and Williams that he had found the Lord and was going to make something of himself when he got out.

David Kesterson served eight calendar years in prison before he died of a brain aneurism. Judy "Brandy" Gonzling served two and a half years of her ten-year sentence for burglary of a habitation before she was paroled. Don Broyles would have to serve ten years before he came up for parole for the first time.

This was not an "And they all lived happily ever after" story but the guilty parties all hit the crossbar hotel for several years.

•THE DIRTY END OF THE STICK•

Al Cuellar was a Texas Ranger working in the counties around the San Antonio, Texas area. He started his career with the state police working in eastern Texas where family trees often do not fork. His promotion to Ranger brought him back to south Texas and the area north of San Antonio known as The Hill Country. Some refer to The Hill Country as a place where men are men and sheep are nervous. In the Rangers, Cuellar worked with police and sheriff's departments throughout that area. In this case, he came in after the fact (a few days later) on a cattle theft in a county north and west of San Antonio. At the time he was one of the few Spanish-speaking Rangers in the state.

The cattle theft occurred in a rural section of Wilson County, and when Cuellar entered the picture, the local sheriff's department had no leads. The owner of the animals was a local Bohemian with a Polish last name that most of the locals could not pronounce, so they just called him Ski. Ski showed the Ranger evidence the thieves had pulled into his property, rounded the cows into the loading pen, and then ran them through the loading chute into a trailer and simply hauled them off. Getting cattle into a pen usually only takes some feed or range cubes on gentle stock, and a cattle prod will push them in most any direction from there–steps a basic cattle thief could easily accomplish. Anyway,

Cuellar went to the theft site and spoke with Ski and looked over the property. He noticed a mesquite tree that stood beside the loading chute, and it appeared a large branch been broken off—and recently, judging from the condition of the bark—but no limbs lying on the ground. Cuellar made note, then began searching for possible witnesses.

He started a circular search of the area, stopping and visiting with local residents about any trucks with stock trailers they may have seen in the area around the time of the theft. He spoke to area stockmen and got a general description of a truck and a trailer that had been seen. (Cattlemen take notice of trucks and trailers and such, and as a group are prone to cuss and discuss the merits of one or another brand or style of equipment.) Cuellar was able to get a description of a truck and trailer seen hauling cattle in the general area during the time of the theft. His next step was to question area residents who might know someone with that type and color of truck and trailer. Several residents said that the vehicle and trailer matched the description of those belonging to a local veterinarian. Cuellar then drove to the veterinarian's office and found a truck and stock trailer matching the description he'd been given. Cuellar looked inside the trailer and saw some broken-off pieces of tree limb that had been stomped down into some fresh cow dung. While Cuellar was looking around, the vet came out and they discussed the theft, and the Ranger asked if he'd heard anything about it. The vet said he'd heard it occurred but knew no real particulars. Cuellar asked him if he would mind if he collected the broken tree branches that lay on the trailer floor. The vet laughed and said he was welcome to them, and if he wanted to clean the trailer out he could take anything else he found there with him.

Cuellar went back to the theft site and compared the

broken tree limb sections from the trailer to the tree on Ski's property, and they looked like a match to him. He then cut a broken sample limb from the tree and took both limbs to the crime lab of the San Antonio Police Department. The crime lab techs did a microscopic examination and reported that the sections of the tree limb recovered from the stock trailer had indeed come from the same tree as the sample limb, and that the break from the trailer branch came about due to a specific type of fracture. Their conclusion was that all pieces of limb submitted had come from the same tree branch.

Cuellar's next move was to go back out and knock on doors in an attempt to glean some more information about the vet in question. In Cuellar's world, computers were okay, but knocking on doors and talking to people were how cases got cleared. He focused first on area cattlemen because they all have three things in common. They all need grass, water and good fences. Cattlemen know who has property for lease, and generally who has property leased from whom. And, cattlemen compete for pasture leases, and always are looking for available leases to keep as a hedge against the lurking drought conditions that plague south Texas on a regular basis. If the grass dries up and you are forced to feed out cattle on hay early in the year, your expected profits will quickly evaporate.

Cuellar learned that the animal doctor had grazing rights on three parcels of land. He then went by Ski's house and took him and his son to look at the cow herd he'd located on some land the vet had under lease. When the men pulled up in sight of the herd, the rancher's son piped up from the back seat right away. "Look Paw, there's old Mamu and Daisy Mae. The Ranger's done found our cows!" Cuellar found it hilarious that they had named their cows.

Other lawmen later wondered a bit whether the younger Ski had a possible romantic interest in some of the bovines. Like in the old sonnet: "They lingered beside the garden gate and did not speak. They knew their love was not to be. For he was but a farm boy, and she a Jersey cow."

The local veterinarian was charged with felony theft of the livestock and received a probated sentence on the charge. He qualified for probation since he had no prior arrests and was reputably employed, even if he was a sorry, no-good thief. Following his sentence, the Texas State Veterinary Licensing Board in Austin called Cuellar to testify at a hearing to determine if the vet's license should be revoked. There were several veterinarians seated to hear the case, and a lawyer from the Texas Attorney General's Office acted as the prosecutor. She reviewed the case with the victim and then Cuellar was called. He went over the facts and how he found the broken tree first at the scene and then pieces of limb in the vet's stock trailer. He went into how he submitted them to the crime lab of the San Antonio Police. The prosecutor opened the big evidence envelope and started to reach inside it but then snatched her hand out as if there were a snake inside. She went and got a tissue out of her purse and picked up the tree limb evidence to submit it before the board for review. The thief was allowed to continue practicing veterinary medicine and got six months of licensing probation but was barred from ever owning cattle as long as he kept a valid license to practice his trade in Texas. I guess they figured that might keep him from repeating his cow thieving ways. Who knows.

Some of the local lawmen dubbed Cuellar's investigation "The case of the shitty stick." I thought The Dirty End of the Stick a bit more appropriate for this title.

One final note: Theft of cattle, property crimes, murder,

armed robbery, or most any felony crime all fall under the jurisdiction of the Texas Rangers. Al Cuellar was assigned to Company D of the Texas Rangers, and for many years his captain was named Jack Dean. Dean called his unit "Company Dean" like he owned it. For a time, I suppose he did. Captain Dean said Al Cuellar was like a freight train whenever he was assigned a case–he said when you put him on a track, Al would keep on it until he worked out the case. Jack Dean and Al Cuellar still hold one another in high regard to this day.

•A NON-VIOLENT OFFENDER•

Mary Landry and Tom Messer were two middle-America, suburban-raised kids, high on life. She was nineteen; he was twenty-one and about to wrap up his third year of college at the University of Houston.

One Friday night the couple had gone to a comedy club on their second date. The club was located in Montrose, an area just south and west of downtown. They left the club at eleven–Mary needed to get home, and Tom had an early morning at the local furniture company where he worked on Saturdays doing sales work for pocket money.

As they walked across the parking lot beside the club, the couple was approached by two black males, who were later identified as thirty-five-year-old Leon Rutherford and his seventeen-year-old nephew, Reggie Bateaux. Rutherford had a shotgun and Bateaux carried a .45 caliber Colt automatic pistol. The two armed men forced the couple into a late model, red Ford pickup truck. The captives were forced to sit in the middle of the truck seat with the armed men bracketing them. Rutherford was in the driver's seat and Bateaux sat next to the passenger side door. Mary sat beside Rutherford and noted he had a tattoo—which she later reported looked like a snake—that ran from the point of his elbow almost to his wrist. From the time they left the club

Bateaux kept his pistol shoved up against Tom's ribs. Mary told the men just to take whatever they wanted and let them out. Rutherford responded with an elbow to Mary's face. Needless to say, the victims were cursed and threatened to no end if they did not shut up and do as they were told.

Rutherford had moved to Houston following his latest release from prison. He was from Wharton and Matagorda counties, located west of Houston and along the coast. His three terms in prison were from those two counties, and his convictions, in the order they occurred, were for burglary, forgery, and finally drugs. His sentences were for two, five and three years, respectively. After moving to Houston he had one misdemeanor arrest for theft and at the time of the abduction he was wanted for failing to appear in court while out on bond (posted by his sister).

Rutherford drove the hostages to a vacant government housing project over on the east side of the Third Ward, just on the edge of downtown Houston. The housing project, MacGregor Village, was vacant because it was in the process of being torn down. Rutherford and Bateaux jerked their hostages out of the truck and demanded they put their valuables (including their wrist watches) on the tailgate of the truck. Rutherford was reportedly foaming-at-the-mouth mad because they'd abducted two people with only eleven dollars and sixty-five cents to their names. He butt-stroked Tom Messer in the head and yelled out to his nephew to, "Grab the bitch by the hair and make her watch."

Rutherford then grabbed Tom and dragged him over to the side of the driveway where they were parked and began to pound him in the head with the butt of the shotgun he was carrying. Mary said she could hear the repeated "twock, twock, twock" sound it made every time Rutherford struck Tom's head. After disabling Tom, these two sterling characters both raped Mary. They laughed–and slapped her around repeatedly–as she pleaded for them to stop. When they were done, they put her in the truck, on the seat between them, and drove away, leaving Tom Messer for dead. The pair stopped another time to sexually abuse Mary before literally throwing her out of the truck over on the east side of the district, about two miles from where she was originally abducted.

Mary managed to stumble up to a nearby convenience store where she found an unlocked car in the parking lot, crawled inside, and locked the doors. The clerk on duty spotted Mary in the car, screaming, and called police. Officers Lee Dawson and Ted Thomas responded to the call. Mary was so traumatized that she did not initially recognize Dawson and Thomas as policemen and refused to unlock the car doors. Officer Thomas was able to get the passenger door open, and with some careful reassurance was able to convince Mary who they were and that they were not going to let anyone harm her. Mary begged the officers to go and find Tom, her date, who had been taken captive along with her. She told officers Tom had been beaten in the head and she was afraid he was dead. However, she did not know the location of the vacant housing project and knew nothing about the part of Houston they'd been in.

At first, Mary was crying and screaming and too upset to communicate to the cops who were trying to put the information together.

After she was transported to Ben Taub Hospital, Officer Dawson was able to get the hospital staff to let him take her to a break room to try and interview her, hoping to get enough information for a preliminary report. Once seated at a table, it was as if a switch had been thrown and Mary became the eyewitness of the year. She gave good descriptions of the two men who abducted, robbed and raped her. She was also able to describe the truck that they were driving, even down to the channel that the radio was tuned to. She described the guns and recalled the names the suspects called one another.

Mary was treated by the hospital staff which called in the hospital social worker and contacted Mary's family to take her home. Officer Dawson went to the Central Station, which housed both the Sex Crimes section and Homicide. Dawson advised the Homicide desk about what he had and that they were likely to have a murder scene which was yet to be discovered. He wrote a detailed report and left the deskman a copy.

When the sun came up the next day, the first construction worker to arrive at the housing project site found the battered remains of Tom Messer. Investigators processed the scene and immediately linked it with Dawson's report. Detectives now knew what they had, and where it began and ended. It was obvious to investigators that the two predators had been hunting, and detectives were convinced the pair lived in the area, since they chose a site they knew would be empty and isolated to assault their victims. Mary described the older man as being thirty to thirty-five years old, and the other as being about eighteen. The murder scene itself was more a demolition site than construction site, and as such was covered in debris and trash–a relatively common condition in the Third Ward area.

Later in the day, homicide detectives addressed the 2 p.m. and 3 p.m. Patrol Division roll calls at both the Central and Southeast Stations. They asked the uniformed officers for help in locating the suspects' truck, any possible suspects, or suspect information. Detectives passed along details from Mary on the new single cab Ford truck as well as descriptions of the suspects, down to the snake tattoo on the older man that ran almost from wrist to elbow of his right arm.

Mike Williams worked evenings out of Central and his beat was in the Third Ward. He took the information and began hunting. He stopped several Ford trucks that matched the description, but none contained drivers or occupants that fit the suspects' descriptions. A few hours into his shift, he hit pay dirt. Each time he stopped a truck he would ask the driver if they owned the truck and if anyone other than the driver had use of it. At last, Williams pulled over a truck with a light-skinned driver (the wanted men were dark-skinned) and when the driver was asked if the truck was his he said, "No, it is a rental that belongs to Leon Rutherford." When asked for the rental paperwork, the driver opened the glove compartment and out fell Rutherford's wallet, along with the paperwork on the truck. Officer Williams took down Rutherford's driver's license information, but before he could follow up on the information, he caught a shoplifter call. He sent the driver on his way, and headed to his new dispatch.

After booking the shoplifting thief, Williams went to the Identification Division and picked up a rap sheet and black-and-white picture of Leon Rutherford. The rap sheet included a photograph, which showed a large tattoo of a dagger on Rutherford's right forearm. Williams took the rap sheet down to the Homicide Division and handed it to Detective Jim Binford telling him, "Here's the robbery-homicide rapist you're looking for." Binford told Williams they were currently interviewing the living victim, so Binford immediately ordered a color photo of Rutherford to put in a photo lineup. Williams went back on patrol. Thirty minutes after getting back on the street, Williams got a call on his police radio, advising him that Rutherford had been positively identified by Mary Landry, and for Williams to locate Rutherford and bring him in. Williams immediately assembled a two-man unit, with officers Carpenter and Walls aboard. He showed them the photo of the suspect and was advised that he was supposedly living with relatives in a house on Tuam Street, near Chennault.

Carpenter drove past the house and spotted the red truck–bearing the plates Mike identified as Rutherford's–parked in front of the house. He and Wall set up a surveillance post on a nearby cul-de-sac. Williams sat a block down the street in the opposite direction. Williams had only been in position ten minutes when three kids, ages eleven to thirteen, came out of the suspect's possible location and were all peeking inside the red truck through the side windows. After a few moments, they all turned and walked down the street toward Williams' position. Thinking they looked suspicious, Williams stopped all three kids, patted them down, and searched them for weapons. Then he put them in the back seat of his patrol car. The kids were nervous, but there again, what kids wouldn't be? Williams collected names and home phone numbers from all three, and one of the kids gave his address as the house where the red truck was parked. When asked who he lived there with, the young man said he lived with his grandmother. Williams turned the kids loose and told them not to be prowling around, looking in cars if they did not want to be suspected of criminal activity.

Just after turning the trio loose, Leon Rutherford walked out of the same house. The cops pounced upon him and searched him for weapons. Rutherford refused to permit the cops to search his rented truck and told them to get a warrant. While waiting for detectives to secure a warrant, Williams searched Rutherford's person and found in his right sock—about the level of his outside ankle bone—a torn piece of paper. That paper was from an envelope out of Mary's purse. While stealing belongings from Mary's purse, Rutherford had found an envelope and tore her mailing address off of it, telling Mary he now knew where she lived and that he would kill her if she told anyone what they'd done to her. As it turned out, the tattoo on Rutherford's arm was an Arabian style dagger with the point upswept like a snake's tail. Rutherford was carted to jail, and once detectives had secured a warrant, the red Ford truck was towed to the HPD fingerprint stall for processing.

At the end of his shift, Williams was directed to call Homicide. Detectives had picked up the three kids William had questioned earlier, and one confessed to stealing a watch from Rutherford while visiting the house where Rutherford had been staying. The kid told detectives he had taken the watch off his wrist and shoved it between the back seat cushions of Williams' patrol while he was questioning them. Williams searched his patrol car and found the watch, just where the kid said he'd put it. The watch belonged to Mary. Details of the case now all dove-tailed together.

Mary appeared at Rutherford's trial, and until that day had not seen the crime scene photos. When she was on the stand testifying, she was shown the photos. She reacted with a blood-curdling scream that could be heard throughout the whole third floor of the courthouse. Those photos dragged up horrors she would see in her dreams for the rest of her life.

I once processed a black male murder suspect who was a true hater. He hated white people with all of his being. The man was arrested on a murder warrant for killing his former employer in a robbery. He told me that killing a peckerwood (white person) would never bother him or make him lose sleep. I asked him if he had so much hate, was he also a rapist specializing in white women. He said he would never do that to anyone, because killing someone was one thing, but to ruin their life and haunt their inner spirit was something completely different. To this day I think the hater was telling the truth and that he knew what he was talking about regarding sexual assault victims.

Rutherford had previously been convicted of capital murder and given the death penalty. That conviction was overturned because the judge did not, in the jury's charge, allow the fact to be included that a life sentence was worth twenty calendar years in prison before eligibility of parole.

Rutherford was convicted of capital murder in the death of Tom Messer, and once again given the sentence of the death penalty. His co-defendant was certified to stand trial as an adult due to his extensive arrest record as a juvenile. He was given a life sentence.

Tom Messer's parents were both in their early sixties when they lost their only child in an armed robbery. Messer was killed by a three-time ex-convict for a total of $11.65. Messer's parents sat through the trials of both defendants, in their entirety. Neither parent said a word until the trials were over when they went forward and thanked the jurors for their findings.

The defense attorney during the punishment portion of the trial kept harping on the fact that Rutherford had never been convicted of, or even been arrested for, a violent crime. He claimed it was not Rutherford's nature to be violent. Ask any detective if he has arrested murder suspects with lengthy property crime or drug offenses who went on to commit capital murder, and every detective will tell you he has. It is in their nature if they are criminals, particularly if they are drug users.

At the time of the last trial, Mary Landry had married and was living in Chicago with her husband and two children. Leon Rutherford was finally put to death in Huntsville, Texas on Mike Williams' birthday. (By the way, capital punishment is the only rehabilitation process that so far has a 100 percent success rate.)

This story is very dark, but shows that good police work on the street level can bring about exceptional results. Williams would work for two other police agencies along the Texas Gulf coast before retiring. A crook once told him, "Williams, you're not the smartest detective in the world, but you're just like a damned pocket gopher and just won't stop digging once you start." In police work, that's what it takes.

Lee Dawson also went on to work for two other police agencies and is now retired.

Without the quality of their work this case may not have turned out as well as it did. This is a career case, and at times it still stirs emotion in those who worked it–not just the innocent victims and their families.

Real men have trouble explaining this sort of thing to outsiders.

•THE LONG ARM OF THE PA•

For a time, strip club businesses in both Houston and Dallas were dominated by the Greeks—mostly a mixture of old-country guys who married US citizens and first-generation Americans. This story is about one Greek who was not smart enough to run like hell when he had the chance.

Nicholas Kaludus was the owner and operator of a high-end men's club off Houston's Southwest Freeway, just a few miles north of downtown. His stable of dancers consisted of pretty young women, many of whom were heavy drug users. They worked for Kaludus because he had a direct pipeline to any kind of drug anyone would ever want, reportedly the best drugs to be had anywhere. He never sold drugs, nor did he allow any to be sold in his place. If anyone tried to do sell there, they were dealt with by a couple of steroid-freak knuckle-draggers that worked for him. Problem children were sent packing or crawling off if they got mouthy or moved too slow. Kaludus liked to snort a little cocaine from time to time, but supplying his girls was his main thing. The ladies got a good product and their purchases were deducted from their paycheck. Kaludus was all business. He did not mix business with pleasure, nor would he discuss anything illegal on a telephone. Then one day, Monica showed up.

Monica Day came into the club looking for a job. She'd worked in Las Vegas, Nevada, but had just returned to Houston after a year's absence. She said her family was in Houston and she wanted to be closer to them than three to four hours by plane. She was twenty-three years old and movie star pretty. Kaludus fell in love on the spot.

Monica played up to Kaludus and moved into his home within a week of their first meeting. She would take care of his every need, day or night. She also had a tremendous capacity to ingest drugs but continue to function pretty much normally. Kaludus kept her stoned and bought her pretty things. She really enjoyed smoking cocaine cut with a pinch of heroin. Another favorite of hers was cooking heroin in a spoon and sniffing the fumes that came off of it–a process known as *chasing the dragon*.

When Monica moved into Kaludus' high-rise apartment, her dad came by the club to pay him a visit. Daddy was a Texas state district court judge and rough old man in his own right. At nineteen, he won a bronze star in combat and while on the bench he'd shot and killed someone stupid enough to try and rob him in a parking lot outside a restaurant. Dear Old Dad was point-blank with Kaludus, as he was about everything else in life. He told Kaludus that Monica had a drug problem and that he understood Kaludus kept high-end strippers around by supplying those pathetic women with good-quality drugs. Judge Day went on to say that Monica had just recently gotten out of a drug rehab program and that if Kaludus put her in a tailspin by feeding her dope that he (Kaludus) would not live to regret it. Kaludus launched into a macho man routine by yelling, "You don't come into my place telling me what to do and---." His tirade ended abruptly when Daddy stood up very quickly, from the far side of Kaludus' desk, and put a .357

under the Greek's nose. He then eared back the hammer. Daddy then asked quietly, "Can you remember what I just said, asshole?" Kaludus' only comment was, "Yes, sir."

Unfortunately for Nick Kaludus, he either did not take Judge Day seriously enough, or he thought he was smarter than him. It is doubtful that he thought His Honor was kidding. After a night of partying and making whoopee with his lady love, Kaludus and Monica fell into a drug-induced slumber. Kaludus awoke with an erection and reached for the girl who never said no. However, Monica was dead as a hammer and stiff as a carp.

After the initial shock wore off, Kaludus shifted into survival mode. He called a dirty, alcoholic cop named Johnny Z. Johnny came right over and helped clear the place of any traces of drugs, hauling off one ounce of cocaine and various other controlled substances. To top it off, Johnny concocted a pretty good story for Kaludus to lay on the cops when they arrived. "I am in love with this beautiful girl. She was heavily into drugs when I met her and I have been trying to get her clean and off of them completely. She may have gotten ahold of some dope at work yesterday from one of those bitches there. I just don't know." When the cops were called they went over the place with everything but a vacuum cleaner. They even brought in a drug dog. The dog was interested in a couple of areas, but no drugs were found.

Monica's autopsy indicated her cause of death was a cocaine overdose. There were also traces of heroin in her system, but not enough to kill her. Her father claimed her remains from the Harris County Morgue. Kaludus showed up at the funeral, in the company of a couple of Monica's former coworkers. After the services, Judge Day walked up to Kaludus and said, in front of several witnesses, "It may be six days, six months or six years, but with God as my witness I will send you to Hell ahead of me."

Kaludus may well have survived if he'd returned to Greece. At the very least, it would have been a whole lot harder to find him on the island of Patmos. As it was, Kaludus chose to relocate to Dallas. About a year after Monica's death, Kaludus walked out of his new strip joint at 3:15 one morning and was shot to death as he walked up on his car. Seven .45-caliber shell casings were found in the area around his body.

The specific procedure used to send Nicky Kaludus to Hell is called *buttoning someone's shirt*–you simply put a bullet in every spot on someone's shirt where a button normally would appear. It really makes no difference if your shots begin just about belt buckle height and go north or if you start at the sternal notch and go south. Either way, you are likely to be standing over them for the last few rounds. If your goal is to put the party down as quickly as possible, you should put you first round just above where you figure his pubic hair will start. The pelvic bone is the heaviest one in the body and when it gets struck it tends to knock people off their feet. (This study into the practical application of terminal ballistics is pretty much unknown outside the world of triggernometry and only to a select number of shootists.)

Satisfaction with this practice is pretty much guaranteed when properly applied. In the words of my later father, "In some areas it is far better to give than to receive."

•MY MOTHER WOULD NEVER FORGIVE ME•

I worked out of the Beechnut Station a couple of times for maybe three or so years while I was working uniformed patrol. During that time my duty hours were generally on the evening shift from 3 p.m. to 11 p.m. There was a night shift criminal investigator I saw on a regular basis named Andrew Wesley who came on at eleven at night. I had no direct dealings with him, but knew that Andy was a close associate of a smart-mouthed cop named James Bruin. I did not care much for Bruin. As such, I wrongfully lumped Wesley into Bruin's class. Guilt by association I guess you might call it.

I had been in the Robbery Division for about a year when Wesley got promoted to detective. I heard he was to be coming to Robbery and was slated to be in my squad. I approached my lieutenant, Don Miller, and told him I'd known Andy Wesley from patrol days and if it was all the same to him, I'd rather not ride with the man. It appeared my lieutenant did not care to be told how to run his squad because Wesley was assigned to be my regular partner and he and I even shared the same days off. I would come to find out that Lt. Don and Wesley were good friends and he knew the two of us had a lot in common. Wesley showed up on his first day as a detective and first went into the captain's office and then directly went into Lieutenant Miller's office. He then walked into the central work area and shook hands with me. Things got really interesting in a hurry.

Wesley told me that he had a sorry drug addict for a brother named Byron. Brother Dear had not been out of prison but for maybe a month and was back to using heroin and stealing from every known family member and their friends. Wesley said that Byron was running with some badass who shot it out with the police the last time anyone tried to arrest him. My new partner had been in touch with both his brother's parole officer and the parole board. Byron's parole had been revoked, at the request of his family, because he had failed to report upon release. Wesley handed me a recent picture of his brother that was taken at his mother's house two weeks earlier. He said he had cleared it with the captain and lieutenant for us to go hunt his brother down. Then he told me, "Byron may be armed, I don't know. And the guy with him is dangerous. If it comes down to a shootout, I want you to kill my brother. If I do it, my mother would never forgive me." We stopped by my house on the way out and I picked up a spare pistol.

My daddy taught me that drawing a second loaded weapon was faster than any reload you could make. Ah, the things I learned during childhood at my dear old father's knee. I guess my early life was different in Ethiopia than it would have been here in Middle America. That or the fact that Dad had been in both World War II and Korea may have had something to do with it. He also told me, "Sometimes it's better to have to read over others from the good book than it is to have someone read over you from it. From this they shall come to judge the quick and the dead."

Anyway, we ran up on Brother Byron and Billy Badass and had no problems taking Stupid into custody on his revocation warrant. We unfortunately could not find a reason to arrest his running buddy. However, the alleged bad-news-companion of the wayward brother was arrested two weeks later on a burglary charge, oddly enough by the same detective who'd shot and wounded him when he decided to act like some kind of pistolero. Wesley's junkie of a brother would be in and out of prison for the next thirty years. His mother would die and she left the junkie a trust that had about a million or so dollars in it. He is still using heavy drugs to this day. The day that he becomes rehabilitated is the day his heart stops pumping. Some people are living proof that cockroaches are hard to eliminate once they get entrenched.

Andrew Wesley and I are still good friends, and our lieutenant was right that we had a lot in common. Andy has told me on several occasions he regrets we were not in a position to send his brother to the great beyond on that day. An interesting aside to this whole story is that when Andy was a brand new rookie he walked into the police station and saw a picture on the bulletin board of his darling younger brother coming out of a savings and loan with a pistol in his hand. He and his training officer went to Andy's mother's house that day and arrested Byron for armed robbery. You just thought you had a dysfunctional family. In police work you figure out that everybody does, and anyone who says otherwise is likely a liar.

•NO HUMAN INVOLVEMENT•

The people your parents warned you about are real. There are those who are completely without morals, and lacking any conscience. Where they come from, the terms "good" or "justified" simply refer to things that have something in it for them. They do not live a life-oriented world. Their American dream does not include a house with a picket fence, two cars, kids and a dog in the yard. This subculture of dangerous individuals rates their priorities as money, sex, drugs, and rock and roll. Money ranks highest of all, because with it everything else can be purchased. The relative worth of a person to these individuals is gauged on their ability to produce drugs, money, sex, or some other asset for which there may be a need or market.

Welcome to the world of drug dealing and the sorry excuse for human beings that run in those distribution and social circles. The players are all the same whether the product is weed, meth or cocaine. Drug users will give you a blank stare if you try to impress upon them that with every joint they smoke or illicit drug they take they line the pockets and encourage people to whom killing, maiming and torture are just a normal part of doing business.

Unfortunately, the only fictional part of this story is the names of the suspects and witnesses. The rest is completely true.

I'm going to introduce you to the misguided individuals that brought this story to light. Had they not been pressured to do so, none of them would have come forward to right a wrong or tell the truth. The murder of Mitchell Rhuby (pronounced Ruby) did not bother any of them in the least. This is common in their world; death is a way of life and simply the cost of doing business in the world of subhuman, dirtbag dopers. Police often call drug-related killings "OSHA cases." You see, if you deal drugs or hang around those that deal drugs, getting killed is just an occupational safety hazard. Sometimes homicide investigators might also label such killings as NHI cases–no human involvement. There is no human involvement regarding the suspects, victims, or most of witnesses in these cases. Sometimes, however, stray gunfire will wound or kill an innocent party.

Now, meet the players in this story.

Mitchell "Mitch" Rhuby: White male, twenty-seven years of age. Served one year of a three-year prison sentence for the burglary of a drug store. Other arrests for DWI and firearms violations. A north side Houston drug dealer dealing in cocaine and methamphetamine with contacts in a couple of motorcycle gangs.

Mark Hershel: White male, twenty-eight years old. North side Houston drug dealer specializing in methamphetamine sales. Criminal charges include carrying a pistol, a misdemeanor marijuana charge, and one felony drug possession charge which got him a three-year probated sentence.

Darleen (Darla) Maresh (pronounced Marsh): White female, twenty-five years old. Worked as a dancer in totally nude clubs. Arrests in Houston and Los Angeles for prostitution. Bi-sexual and a heavy drug user.

Beverly (Big Girl) Scruggs: White female, thirty-six years old. Served thirteen months of a three-year sentence for robbery by assault. Warehouse manager for a large food chain. Male counterpart in a relationship with witness Suzy Sizemore.

Suzanne (Suzy) Sizemore: White female, twenty-six years old. Worked as either a barmaid or a waitress. Roommate and lover of witness Big Girl Scruggs. Criminal history of drunken driving, shoplifting, and assault with bodily injury.

This unusual case began with "the magic phone call." Sergeant Doug Osterberg was working the front desk in Houston's Homicide Division and happened to be the one answering the phone. There are regular desk officers assigned during the week, but on weekends, one of the regular crew of investigators would be drafted to do desk duty for a day. They spoke with patrol officers, did paperwork on prisoners, spoke to victims, family members and the media. Desk men never speak with happy individuals. Welcome to the knife-and-gun club.

Homicide is a catch-all kind of place, and open twenty-four hours. You deal with everything from would-be mystery writers to victims and crazies who want to talk with somebody. The night this case got rolling was simply Doug's night in the barrel.

This case began with a call from the Detective Bureau of the Baltimore, Maryland police department. They had a female in their offices claiming to be a witness to a five-year-old murder in Houston. The woman claimed to be a former Houston resident who walked into Baltimore's Sex Crimes Unit, claiming she had been abducted and sexually assaulted by an ex-convict named Mark Hershel. She further advised them she was an eyewitness to Mark Hershel killing another drug dealer named Mitchell Rhuby six years earlier in Houston. She told investigators she not only witnessed the killing but lived with Hershel for almost eighteen months after he'd committed the murder.

After collecting the information from the Baltimore investigator, Doug first checked HPD's computer system and found a missing person report listing Mitchell Rhuby as missing in action. The report was generated by his mother and remained open. A quick call to Rhuby's mother verified he was still missing and she feared he was dead, as family was a priority in his life. She said that before he went missing five years ago, he called her every other night at seven o'clock without fail.

Doug called the Baltimore detectives back and they advised him of their situation. The alleged victim, Darleen Maresh, walked into their Sex Crimes office making allegations of being abducted from her apartment complex parking lot by a known suspect. She worked as a totally nude dancer in clubs in Baltimore. She said Hershel grabbed her from her apartment parking lot and took her in his car to a motel in their city. He kept her in his motel room overnight and had his way with her sexually. While he was asleep, she got up and put on her clothes and went straight to the police station. Her main concern was that he had found her and she was afraid of him. Baltimore PD had been in contact with their own district attorney's office which was not interested in filing charges. Patrol officers were sent to check the "no tell" motel but Hershel was gone upon their arrival.

The Baltimore DA knew that totally nude clubs were nothing but fronts for houses of ill repute, and that the complainant had two prior arrests for prostitution. Prostitutes regularly claim rape when there is a problem with payment for services rendered, so this victim was not highly credible.

The main reason Baltimore PD cops were calling Houston investigators was because of the uncleared homicide case information Maresh wanted to pass along. Doug asked to speak directly to Maresh and she related a series of facts about Rhuby's murder by Hershel.

Maresh had been living with Mitch Rhuby in a rented townhouse at the time of his killing. She split living expenses with him and described their relationship as being "roommates with benefits." Rhuby was a north Houston drug dealer and Mark Hershel was an associate of his, also a heavy drug dealer. They really were not competitors as they lived and worked in different portions of Houston's north side. The "lady in question" admittedly was involved sexually with both Rhuby and Hershel at the same time, a situation unknown to Rhuby. Both men sold good quality drugs and that was Maresh's attraction to both of them. It appeared she was a woman in need of stimulation, and did not care much if it as chemically or mechanically produced.

When Doug Osterberg spoke with Maresh she was matter-of-fact about living with Rhuby while she was having a side relationship with Mark Hershel. She said she never told Rhuby about she and Hershel having sex, but there again she never talked about turning tricks at work, either. Business was business, and she was (in her own her words) "a part of the sex industry." Hershel came over one evening and the three of them were drinking a few beers. There was no discord or arguing, and suddenly Hershel pulled out a revolver and shot Rhuby several times. Maresh said she freaked out, ran out of the house and into a townhouse two doors down where some acquaintances named Suzy Sizemore and Beverly Scruggs lived. It would later come out that Maresh was also sexually involved with these two ladies.

About an hour after the shooting the three women decided to go back to Hershel and Maresh's townhouse. When they walked in, they were greeted warmly by Hershel. Mark Hershel had found Rhuby's stash of meth and offered to share it with the ladies. The dope Rhuby had on him was methamphetamine produced by the Pagans biker gang and it was famous. Pagan Purple was wholesaled by the gang, and sold only to select dealers. Their brand of dope was usually cut so many times that it turned white when peddled at street level. The funny thing about meth users is that they don't know that dealers cut their speed with a white powdered baby laxative. The dopers can snort a line of speed and have to run to the john in short order. They will tell you, "Man that stuff is so strong it will literally knock the shit right out of you." Little do they know.

The three misguided women and the illicit pharmaceutical salesman sat around Rhuby's townhouse, shooting the dead man's speed for a day and a half. Rhuby had been rolled up in an area rug and was lying on the vinyl floor in the utility room. After a while he began to stink pretty badly so Hershel came up with a plan to dispose of his former associate (and competitor for the affection of the lovely Darleen Maresh). Hershel decided that he needed to haul the body out of the townhouse. He hit on a plan and drafted Beverly Scruggs to help him. Beverly was called "Big Girl" because she was just that. She was a big old gal, not just fat, but built like a linebacker. Hershel told Beverly he needed her help to dispose of Rhuby. He went to the garage and opened the trunk of Rhuby's car, and with the help of Big Girl they put him inside. Then the two loaded up and drove west on Highway 290 toward Austin. After they'd passed Brenham–a couple of hours outside Houston–the body in the trunk really got to stinking badly. A short while later,

Big Girl told Hershel the funk was about to make her puke. Hershel pulled over at a barbeque restaurant, handed her a $50 bill and told her to drink a couple of beers and have some lunch. She did and he drove off, returning in about an hour.

When he picked her up, Hershel told her he had gotten rid of Rhuby, and they drove back east toward Houston with the windows down. Near Brenham (again) the stink overwhelmed the both of them. They found a self-service car wash in Brenham and pulled over to do some cleanup, and hopefully get rid of the smell. There, Hershel opened the trunk and Big Girl saw tissue, and what she took to be guts, in the trunk's interior. Hershel pulled the trunk liner out and threw it into a dumpster at the car wash. Then he washed down the inside of the trunk with soap and water. Big Girl later reported that the fender wells were pretty full of the nasty water so Hershel used a hammer and a large, flat-bladed screwdriver to poke holes in the lower part of the fender wells. He did so to drain some of the water off so it did not short out the car's electrical system on the way back to Houston. He did not want to risk the brake lights going out, and attracting undo attention. (By all rights there should have been a line of turkey vultures following the car up and down Highway 290.) After cleaning the car, Big Girl and Mark went back to Houston's north side and the involved parties all went about their lives as normal. The normal side of life to this group differs from that of most people, thankfully.

Big Girl and her live-in, Suzy, went about their daily routines and Maresh moved in with Hershel since Rhuby was no longer in the picture. Maresh had lived with Rhuby for about ten months prior to his demise, and she co-habitated with Hershel for a little over a year before he was arrested and charged with two counts of aggravated (armed) robbery and sentenced to five years in prison. Maresh, as usual, landed on her feet (or maybe her back) and went on to ply her trade. She eventually wound up in Baltimore, Maryland where Hershel caught up with her after being released from prison. He told her that he was now living in Phoenix, Arizona and wanted her to join him there and resume their old relationship. She was not interested in that and wanted the cops to get him out of her world.

After Maresh recalled her story, Doug Osterberg advised her that he was going to have to run this all past his supervisors before he could promise to do anything in this case. The captain of the division gave the go-ahead for Doug, also known as Big Bird by his fellow investigators, to fly to Baltimore and get a sworn statement from Darleen Maresh. She agreed to appear before a grand jury in Houston, if required for prosecution purposes.

With a detailed affidavit from the cause of the killing, Doug went and looked up the lesbians to get statements from them. Beverly Scruggs was forthcoming with her knowledge in the case but Suzy Sizemore was not. She said she did not want to get involved in anybody else's business like this. Doug took the case to the Special Crimes section of the Harris County District Attorney's office. He met with a prosecutor there named Ted Wilson and the two discussed the problem of trying to convict a suspect of murder without a body or any physical evidence. The adage in Texas used to be "No body—no crime." But Wilson did some research on the law and it stated that the jury had to believe that the victim was dead, but the presence of a cadaver or some sort of remains was not specifically required. Further, he found there had been a case out of Dallas where a suspect was convicted without a body, so Wilson opted to take this case before a grand jury. All three witnesses testified when subpoenaed. Suzy Sizemore did so reluctantly. When handed her subpoena–while waiting tables in a bar–she knocked her subpoena to the floor and yelled out, "Everybody look! I never touched it so I've not been served." She was advised that if she refused service that the district attorney could file a writ of detainer and she could wait to testify while sitting for a week or two in the Harris County Jail. She picked up the subpoena from the floor.

A grand jury, upon review of the facts and after hearing testimony, returned a true bill against Mark Hershel, indicting him for murder. All three witnesses told the truth about the dope and their actions. Hershel was arrested in Arizona and brought back to Houston for trial.

When trial time came about six to eight months later, all three of the ladies showed up. The day before the trial, Big Girl Scruggs dropped a minor bomb shell. At the end of the pretrial preparation session, she told Ted Wilson, "I gotta tell you something. I lied about something when I went before the grand jury." Wilson was shocked and found out that she'd been asked if she took anything of the dead man's after his murder. During her ride-along trip up towards Austin, Hershel told Big Girl that he had taken the dead man's cash as well as his meth, and he gave Scruggs a one hundred dollar bill for helping him with the body.

All parties involved (except the defendant) testified at the murder trial and were pretty well raked over by defense attorney, Larry Dowell, someone Ted Wilson described as both a good man and a very capable lawyer. Big Girl was pounded pretty hard about lying to the grand jury, but she said she had told the whole truth at trial time. She knew she could be prosecuted but she was not going to lie during a trial; it was too important. The jury nodded in approval. The mother of Mitchell Rhuby tearfully testified that there was no doubt her son was dead. He was a loving son who called her at seven o'clock every other night to check on her and to visit. The defense passed the witness. You don't try to upstage crying mothers, children or animals.

The defense attorney did a good job during his final arguments. He went into the witnesses' criminal histories, drug use and lifestyles. The most creative thing he did, however, was concerning the fact that nobody could produce the body. The details of this charge were related to the jury. The factor of "beyond a reasonable doubt" was dealt with there. In addressing the jury, Dowell said, "They could not produce the body. The best they could do was bring in a bunch of dopers, ex-cons and deadbeats to lie. Do you want to know where Mitchell Rhuby really is? I can tell you"—and he turned and pointed to the back of the courtroom, saying, "If you turn and look you can see him walking through that door right now." Everybody in court that day turned and looked at the rear doors and, of course, no one entered the courtroom. Then the defense walked up to the jury box and said, "You all looked. There's your reasonable doubt. You all have it because you all looked for him. You all have doubt, and therefore my client must be found not guilty."

The jury did not buy the theatrics and not only found Mark Hershel guilty, but gave him a life sentence. Ted Wilson later defended the conviction before the court of appeals and it was upheld. This was a good piece of work both in the case investigation and again at trial time.

Justice truly was served, even if the victim was a sorry, low-life, scum-sucking dope dealer. Actually, society won twice. A dope dealer was dispatched and no state funds were spent to bury him. Secondly, the dope dealer who dispatched him got a life sentence. The world is a better place.

Some of the skeletal remains of the complainant, Mitch Rhuby, were ultimately discovered. About two years after the murder, and three years before the trial took place, a human skull was discovered in Travis County, Texas. It was that of a white male approximately thirty years of age. It went unidentified for several years and sat in plastic tub in the Travis County Medical Examiner's Office. Rhuby had a sister who lived in Illinois. She entered her DNA into a registry called CODIS, an aconym for Combined DNA Index System, a database maintained and managed by the FBI. The Travis County Sheriff's Department formed a Cold Case Squad and the detective assigned there had the DNA of all unknown persons in the Travis County Morgue loaded into the CODIS system. The skull was finally identified as belonging to Mitchell Rhuby. Hopefully his family got some closure, and the state got some sales tax from a funeral home on his behalf.

This was a case of both good investigation by the cops and good legal work by the Harris County District Attorney's Office. After both Doug Osterberg and Ted Wilson retired from their agencies a certain Homicide sergeant would (while teaching in-service schools on interrogation techniques) claim he had cleared this only murder case in Harris County where no body was ever found. In the words of my late father, "you can't shine shit."

•THEY DIDN'T KILL MUCH•

I was working the four in the afternoon to midnight shift out of Homicide. The night shift came in at eleven–a deliberate scheduling strategy, because by overlapping shifts, overtime pay could be minimized on late murder scenes.

There was an early car on evening shift as well that came in at three in the afternoon. This way, if a late scene dropped, a pair of day shift detectives would not be held over four or five hours. One of the night shift sergeants named Randy Zumwalt stuck his head in my office one evening. I'd known him since he was a rookie patrolman and he rode with me during a training cycle. He stepped in and told me, "I made a murder scene last night where the guy who got killed was married to a cousin of yours." I asked who it had been and was told the dead man's name was Michael Black. My only comment was, "Well, they didn't kill much." Randy burst out laughing and said, "Your uncle called in, said y'all were kin and spoke to me asking if the information about the murder was true. I verified his son-in-law's death and his comment was the exact same as yours: 'Well, they didn't kill much.' Wow, your tribe really thinks along the same lines, don't they? Now I know that there's more than one cold-blooded-son-of-a-priest in your family."

At the time of his death, my relative's husband was out on bond on a felony marijuana charge and for carrying a pistol. He apparently was fooling around with some older woman, and her estranged husband came to his soon-to-be-ex's house, demanding to speak to the soon-to-be-sainted Michael. Hubby called out, "I just want him to look me in the eye." Mike swaggered up to the front door and smirked as he said, "Well, I'm looking at you." The unhappy husband then pulled out a revolver and fired a 148-grain, .38-caliber wadcutter bullet into Mike's left eye. It was an entry-only wound and the projectile remained inside the skull. Saint Michael caught the full brunt of the bullet's hydrostatic shock into his dope-addled brain. He was dead when he hit the floor.

The world was a better place, but there were two unfortunate things that occurred following Michael Black's death. The first was that his funeral expenses were paid (up to the tune of ten thousand dollars) from the Texas Victims of Violent Crime Fund. This organization will pay up to ten grand to bury a worthless soul (such as he), though Michael's carcass really should have been hauled off to a landfill. The second unfortunate detail was that the poor bastard who plugged a worthless, wife-beating, dope-pushing son-of-a-bitch was sentenced to forty years in prison.

If I'd had any idea the shooter's sentence would have been so harsh, I would have testified on his behalf. In a just world, the legal defense expenses of the warthog's husband should have been paid for out of some federal urban renewal funds. Then Saint Michael could have been filed on posthumously for bestiality. To my way of thinking, the shooter's actions simply removed a canker sore from the butt of humanity. Admittedly, I am not an unbiased witness in this matter. Praise the Lord and pass the ammunition.

•YOU CAN'T CLEAR THEM ALL•

On August 18, 1983, Hurricane Alicia made landfall on the Texas Gulf Coast and swirled her way across the city of Houston. A Category 3 storm, Alicia left twenty-three people dead and property damage estimated at $2 billion.

The following day, Houston PD Homicide received a call about a triple homicide at a real estate office in one of Houston's high-rent district. Three more people dead, murdered in cold blood, as Hurricane Alicia was making her way onto land.

The murder scene was inside a one-story real estate office in a Houston's tony residential district called Memorial. The building faced Memorial Drive and had parking areas in front and back. Employees parked behind the business and left the front parking spaces for clients and customers. Behind the main office was a storage building, used mostly to store For Sale signs and such. A total of eighteen agents worked out of that office, coming and going at all hours. This was not a fly-by-night operation.

The owner, and resident agent under whose license the others worked, was Iris Schumann. She and two other women, Linda Black and Pam Myers, were found dead or dying on the floor just inside the main lobby of the business. The woman who discovered the murders was another agent who pulled in about forty-five minutes after the usual closing time, letting herself in by way of the back door. She'd noted three cars, belonging to her fellow agents, parked on the property but thought nothing of it. Upon finding the bodies she ran across the street to another business and had both the police and an ambulance called. Pam Myers was still gurgling and a Life Flight helicopter was called for her. The helicopter landed, and while the medical staff aboard were headed into the building, the chopper's motor died. The pilot could not restart the motor. A second helicopter was called and immediately transported Mrs. Myers to Hermann Hospital, where she died a short time later.

This real estate office handled both sales and rentals of area residences. Because of an oil boom elsewhere, many area property owners temporarily moved out of town following work either elsewhere in the US or overseas. Rather than leave their valuable houses sitting vacant many owners chose to rent their homes out for a year or two, putting their good furniture in storage and donating the rest to charity.

Murders in well-to-do neighborhoods are not the cases of choice for many detectives—they're almost always accompanied by extra pressure to clear them in a hurry. Political pressure will be applied, and investigators are subject to closer-than-normal scrutiny by not only direct supervisors, but from the department command staff as well. In this particular murder case, many Memorial area residents contribute to politicians' campaigns. Enough said.

Ken Johnson and David Calhoun were assigned the scene. They were a pair of men who were like night and day. Both men stood over six feet tall. Johnson was portly and boisterous whereas Calhoun had a lean build and tended to be quieter and laid back. Johnson had dark hair and eyes; Calhoun was blonde and fair-skinned. Johnson came from Louisiana and got into police work after college. Calhoun was from north Texas. Calhoun earned the nickname "Cowboy" because he rode the rodeo circuit before joining the Houston Police Department. He rode that circuit between injuries, that is. (Injury is the price of admission to work in the rodeo arena.) He also wore western boots and his duty weapon sported stag-horn grips. Johnson was a clothes horse and tended to wear black suits, white shirts and expensive ties. Due to his pear-shaped profile Johnson was dubbed "Opus" after the penguin in the Doonesbury comic strip.

And so it began. Due to the neighborhood, and the number of dead people, the crime lab was called in so investigators could minimize the "Why didn't you..." questions that were sure to follow, both from upper management within the division and from "The Brass" who would surely be monitoring the case.

At this point in Houston's history each pair of evening shift detectives made between twenty-five and thirty-eight murder scenes a year. Homicide scenes in Houston are generally split between the two men making the scene—one takes the witnesses and the other does the scene description. In this case, Johnson took the scene and Calhoun the witnesses. There was only one actual witness—Amanda Dickenson, the agent who had found the bodies—so Calhoun helped search the scene for clues after he finished knocking on doors of neighboring businesses, looking for any additional witnesses. After the lady who found the bodies calmed down she gave Calhoun some information regarding the normal procedure around the business, and said that on the day of the murders, the owner stayed behind when everybody left as a group at closing time. Mrs. Schumann told the others she had an overseas call coming in from a homeowner whose property she was managing.

Amanda knew that the other two victims had left together earlier, to go have supper somewhere. Investigators surmised that the ladies returned to the office and stumbled in on a robbery in progress. It was immediately noted that there was a sixteen-foot-length of window sash cord that had been brought into the building by the suspect or suspects. It lay on the carpet beside the body of Iris Schumann. This evidence, among other things, supported the theory of a robbery gone bad, as opposed to a contract killing. Whatever happened, the end result was the same—three dead women.

Often, a scene overview is helpful to figure out a crime scene. At this scene, the three victims' cars were parked in the lot behind the building. A look inside each vehicle told investigators all three cars had been searched. Glove compartments were left open and their contents dumped out. The ransacking of the cars bolstered the theory this was a robbery/homicide because the suspects had obviously been looking for something. This discovery created more work for the crime scene unit and print lab employees. After processing the vehicles, no real identifiers were ever made, which was no big surprise. Murder scenes typically yield little, if any, latent fingerprint evidence.

Other than the car interiors, nothing else appeared to have been moved or touched by the suspect(s). Detectives believed there were at least two suspects because very few people are going to hang around searching cars after they have shot and killed three people. Further, the victims had not been tied up. A lone robber would not leave his victims unattended to go and search their cars.

David Calhoun found one possible witness at a business located across the street and down a couple of lots.

The man told Calhoun that on the day the bodies were discovered, he had seen a dark, full-size sedan parked on a side street that would have had a full view of the real estate office and its single entry and exit driveway. The witness said the car had been parked on the side street, about one hundred feet back from Memorial Drive, at least two hours prior to when the real estate office closed for the day. He did not see the vehicle up close, and could not say whether it was occupied or not. The street it was parked on had undeveloped vacant lots on either side of it for a complete block. Calhoun checked the area where the witness indicated the car had been parked, and found no cigarette butts or trash (cups, cans or bottles) that could be linked—by fingerprints or DNA—to the location and possible suspects.

All three women had been killed in the waiting area up near the front entry door. Iris Schumann had been shot in the side of the head, at the level of her temple. The bullet angled down and exited her neck. The angle of the bullet path—forty-five to fifty degrees—indicated she was likely on her knees when she was shot and killed. The kill shot bullet angles on the other two women indicated they had been forced to lie face down on the floor and held at gunpoint. Linda Black was shot in the back of the head and her hands were under her face as if she had been covering her eyes. The third victim, Pam Myers, was found lying across the body of Linda Black, as if she had gotten up and was trying to flee when shot in the body with an entry-no exit type wound. All three women were shot with the same weapon. All that could be deduced was that two of the women were trying to get up off the floor and make a break for it when whoever was guarding them opened fire, killing all of them.

The business was spotless inside—obviously typical—with nothing out of place. Investigators did note one interesting thing, though. The blinds on the windows looking out over the back parking area were twisted and bent in one spot, as if someone had been looking out of them. That person would have been about 5′10″ tall, as the 6′1″ tall Calhoun had to stoop to about that degree. The blinds themselves had no fingerprints on them, only a wipe mark like cotton gloves would leave behind. It was thought that whoever was robbing the place was looking out the back as Amanda Dickenson drove up. First responders found the front door to be closed and unlocked.

After the crime lab folks had cleared Mrs. Schumann's office, Calhoun began a search of it. The only notation on her desk calendar for the day of the murder was *Linda Williams – 4:30 PM sign paperwork on Perthshire rental house*. Calhoun went through the desk drawers and found nothing of interest. While seated at Iris's desk he kicked a wastepaper basket under her desk. It was completely full of paper that was, for the most part, crumpled up. Calhoun went through every piece or scrap of paper one at the time, reading each and hoping for some sort of clue. About halfway down, he found Iris's purse hidden in the basket. She had obviously camouflaged her purse with paper. Calhoun began searching the purse, pulling out each item, and came to a lumpy cloth eyeglass case with a clasp on one end. He opened it and dumped the contents onto the desktop, which turned out to be jewelry later valued at about one hundred thousand dollars. Motive for a robbery became pretty obvious about that time.

Through interviews with other agents who worked out of that office, investigators learned Mrs. Schumann had done a photo shoot two weeks before, updating photos for ads going into a high-end statewide magazine. In those photos, she was decked out in all of her best jewelry.

The other agents in that office knew she had not returned her valuables to bank safety deposit box where she usually stored them, and in fact, several co-workers had warned her to do so. Iris complained she never seemed to find time for her personal errands because business was so demanding.

Robbery now seemed to be the most likely motive, and a search of the property turned up a fancy diamond dinner ring stuffed between the cushions of the couch in the front entry room, giving further credence to the idea of an armed robbery that went bad. Calhoun and Johnson interviewed the remaining fifteen agents who worked out of that office. Nothing other than the robbery could be found as a motive. The scene was processed, and afterward the detectives went to the medical examiner's office to fill out the autopsy request and charted the victims' wounds for their report.

Only then did the detectives return to the Homicide office for multiple hours of typing of the original offense report. In the early morning hours they called it quits and headed home, agreeing to return to the office at noon. Upon returning the next day, they learned they were now part of a nineteen-man task force working this triple homicide. There were hundreds of leads coming into Homicide and local politicians were getting calls and demands for higher police patrols and security. The Crime Stoppers tip line was also going bonkers.

The task force met every morning and steadily ran down leads. One person was assigned to take inquiries and calls, and pass along any incoming tips and clues to investigators. An astounding number of calls came in that were without basis, among them quite a few anonymous calls made with the sole purpose of creating problems for unrelated people. One caller stated that the husband of one of the dead women set the whole thing up, and documentation could be found in a Tupperware bin, buried next to an unused metal building on a certain street. A detective went out there armed with a shovel and dug up the bin, which contained a note inside it which read, "He's in the mob and she knows too much." That was just one of many outlandish calls. Many were well-intended while others were from crackpots and people claiming to be psychics. Nothing panned out.

When interviewed, each of the surviving fifteen agents was asked if they knew of any unusual events or circumstances in the weeks leading up to the murders. A couple of them said Iris had been dealing with a woman looking to rent a house in the neighborhood, but the woman did not fit the mold of their typical client. Agents described her as hard and drawn, and did not act the part of an upper-income, Memorial-type resident. Neither did she dress well on the two occasions she came into the office. On her first visit, she looked at several houses and came in a second time to fill out a rental application.

Interestingly enough, that person who had filled out a rental application was named Linda Williams, the same person who had no-showed on her 4:30 p.m. appointment with Iris Schumann the day of the murders. A search of office files yielded the Linda Williams rental application. Detectives ran her criminal history and background and learned she was a prostitute on her way down. She was a long-time call girl with an arrest record that ran from Las Vegas to Dallas and Houston. Her later arrests in Houston were not, interestingly enough, in the higher-end hotels or environments. Her most recent arrest in Houston was for a liquor violation, and powdered cocaine had been found in her pocket when arrested. Her current address was almost ten miles west of the murder site, where she rented a small house in a middle-class neighborhood.

Before she could be interviewed, Linda Williams disappeared. It was one of those left-in-the-middle-of-the-night scenarios, leaving behind her furniture and household items. Her landlord had been trying to evict her, and the power had been turned off due to non-payment for services. She was simply missing in action, and there was no indication where she went. She was added to the list of clues that went nowhere, although Calhoun regularly checked her name on a local, state and national level, in the event she re-appeared.

The overseas rental client—the one that Iris Schumann was waiting to speak with the evening she was killed—was located. She told investigators that she was on the phone with Iris and was told, "Hang on for a second, there's somebody at the door." She then heard Iris say, "Oh" and the phone went dead. The client attempted to call back from overseas but no one answered at the business.

The task force ran on for six to eight weeks. Members were pulled off as new murder scenes kept coming in. Calhoun and Johnson went back into the rotation of making scenes and returned to the evening shift, working four in the afternoon until midnight. They made fresh cases and went back to their Memorial Drive case whenever possible. Six months after the initial case, Calhoun did his regular checks for arrests (either Texas or national) and a driver's license check for a change of address on Linda Williams. The driver's license check showed she was reported dead, the reporting agency being the Dade County Florida medical examiner's office. Calhoun called Dade County authorities and was advised there was only one county morgue, the Metro-Dade County Medical Examiner's Office. However, they told Calhoun there had been no Linda Williams logged into their system in the past year. Something stank and it smelled of the witness protection program (technically, the Witness Security Program), run by the U.S. Marshals Service. An inquiry was initiated, through the HPD chief of police's office—by way of a guy who had deep contacts with the United States attorney's office. It produced some answers in about a week. A representative out of the chief's office came down from on high and briefed Johnson and Calhoun. They were told that yes, in fact, the woman in question was in the witness protection program. Secondly, they would not be able to meet her face to face, and could interview her by phone one time only, for only thirty minutes.

People in the witness protection program get new identities and are relocated, usually far away from wherever they lived when entering the program. The reason for this is that participants are likely to be murdered should they remain and testify against someone, or a group, that the United States Attorney wishes to prosecute—typically an organized crime operation. Witness protection participants are given new identities, work histories, and credit histories and can, however, opt to return to their old identities at a later date if they wish.

Ninety-five percent of the people entering the program are criminals who have opted out of prosecution for some crime. They avoid prison by testifying against other criminals that the government is after. This is the U.S. Attorney's office using little fish to catch really big fish. The U.S. attorneys are after what they consider to be real trophy fish—the ones they can hang on the wall, and in doing, so enhance their careers. Witnesses who enter the federal protection program are criminals by nature, and often get arrested under their new names. If you happen to arrest one in your city, your agency will get a call from either the U.S. Marshals Service or the FBI, asking what the person has been arrested for and how much their bond is. You will not be told their real names and background.

In this case, there was no immediate action taken to get an interview with Linda Williams. She could not be tied to the scene, and detectives did not want to use their one shot to hear her say, "Sorry, I don't know what you are talking about"-blowing their chance at talking to her again. Her interview was put on hold until any new information could be found, linking Williams to other possible participants.

The families of the victims were devastated, as were the people who worked with the three victims. Family members of the deceased called regularly, but investigators could provide no new information to help them move on from their losses. Immediately after the murders, many of the other agents quickly wrapped up all pending sales and quit. As a group, they were scared to death, and several of the employees who had worked at Iris Schumann's office even moved out of town.

The case rocked along for approximately two years before any promising leads came in. Ken Johnson promoted to lieutenant and shipped out to another division. Calhoun would pair up with another detective/sergeant named Bob Parish. One day, Calhoun received a call from a Texas prison system captain named Ron Hubbard. Hubbard said there was an inmate at the Darrington Unit who had some information regarding the person who killed the women in Calhoun's triple homicide case. The two detectives made arrangements to interview the inmate.

Fred Curtis was a thirty-something-year-old loser on his second trip through the Texas prison system. This time, he was doing time for felony theft. Curtis told Parish and

Calhoun he had run up on an old running buddy when he was just starting his first round of his second prison sentence. The old buddy was a man named Michael Bouchee (pronounced *boo shay*), and both men were from the Beaumont/Port Arthur area. Curtis crossed paths with Bouchee in a hallway as he was headed to the mess hall. He knew Bouchee was doing time for aggravated robbery out of Jefferson County. They struck up a conversation, and Bouchee told Curtis he was leaving in a few days on a furlough, and that he had a "big lick" lined up at a real estate office in Houston. About that time, a guard broke up their conversation and sent them in different directions. Curtis said that was the last time he had seen or talked to Bouchee. Curtis said he wondered why anyone would do an armed robbery at a real estate office, knowing that type of business did not keep money on hand, and nobody paid cash for a house, not directly to them anyway.

The inmate said it was only a matter of days after crossing paths with his old hometown friend that a hurricane hit the southeast Texas Gulf Coast and everybody was keeping up with it on television. The day after the hurricane hit there was a lot of coverage of the storm damage, followed by the story of three women killed during a robbery at a real estate office in a high-rolling part of Houston. Curtis said he knew right then that was the "lick" that Mike Bouchee mentioned pulling off in Houston.

The detectives wanted to take a sworn affidavit regarding what Curtis had just told them, but Curtis refused immediately, saying, "Not only no, but Hell no." He told the cops that Bouchee was a big, strong Gulf Coast redneck and also a member of the Aryan Nation. He knew Bouchee or his friends would kill him (Fred) in a heartbeat once his name showed up on the probable cause statement on an arrest warrant. Curtis explained that his motivation for talking was the Crime Stoppers reward money.

Curtis said he did not want to walk out of prison this time wearing Salvation Army clothes with only a hundred dollars in cash, a sack lunch and bus ticket home. Curtis admitted he was telling what he knew for the chance to pick up some money he was going to need in a couple of months. Bouchee was still in prison at this time. He had been on furlough at the time of the killing, but did not report back at the end of his furlough. He was a fugitive for six weeks before he was re-arrested while riding as a passenger in a stolen car. Calhoun and Parish thanked the captain who had passed along the information and lined up their interview. He told the detectives he would check around with their Gang Intelligence Unit and see if they could drum up some information on Bouchee.

A week later, Captain Hubbard came through for them once more. It seems that Michael Bouchee was sponsored into the Aryan Brotherhood by another inmate, Roland Harris. Harris was doing three life sentences for a crime spree he was involved in that ended in a shootout with police out of Silsbee, Texas. Harris was a honcho in the Aryan Brotherhood and reputedly still ran a bunch of the operation by coded letters and communications with his lawyer, which by law could not be monitored. He also (supposedly) had links to the outside world through some underpaid guards who were not opposed to picking up a few hundred dollars for placing a few calls or mailing letters. Harris was housed in a high-security unit in Brazoria County, south of Houston. The detectives secured an interview with Harris, but in an unconventional setting. Captain Hubbard drove the detectives into the complex in a prison system car and bypassed the normal check-in procedure. They went to a side building that was completely empty and were ushered into an office furnished with only a desk and two chairs. The chairs faced one another across the desk.

Through a side window in the office, the investigators were able to see Roland Harris being escorted out of the main building by a guard, and walked toward the cinder-block unit where the detectives were waiting. Harris was about five feet ten inches tall, and weighed in at about three hundred pounds. He was muscled up like a champion pit-fighting dog, with tattoos covering his neck and both arms, running down onto his hands. He looked just like the leader of a white supremacy prison and drug gang was supposed to. As Harris entered the building Calhoun looked over at Parish and told him, "If he comes across this table and grabs me by the throat just shoot me, because I'm sure it will be faster than dying from a crushed windpipe." Parish did not laugh.

Harris turned out to be a pretty decent guy to deal with. Calhoun was up front with him about everything. He told Harris, "I am not going to lie to you and promise you a bunch of stuff I can't produce. I am working a triple homicide and I have reason to believe that a man you sponsored into the Aryan Brotherhood murdered three women in Houston during an armed robbery."

The inmate listened intently and told the investigators that he wanted to hear it all. Roland admitted bringing Bouchee into the Brotherhood and having known him for a long time. He also said he did not agree with murdering women, or needlessly killing any white person, for that matter. Then he brought forward a plan. He said that if Mike Bouchee killed those women, he had no problem giving him up. The problem as he saw it, though, was that he knew nothing about the event. The gang leader told them that if they put him and Bouchee together in the same unit, he was sure Bouchee would tell him all about it if he had been involved in their case.

After the interview the detectives followed up with Captain Hubbard. He said that the transfers were possible, but that the inside of a prison was like a very small town, and it would have to be done in a manner that would not be obvious. The approach least likely to arouse suspicion would be to conduct multiple transfers, and include Harris and Bouchee in the mix, but a task that could take several months to pull together. To transfer one inmate is one thing. To shuffle ten to thirty, when multiple transfers were being done between units, was quite another.

The transfers that brought Bouchee and Harris together took three months. Unfortunately, the new arrangement did not last long. Harris had been in the same unit with Bouchee a total of two days when another inmate heard some others discussing that a rival prison gang had marked Roland Harris for death. He informed the Bosses (guards) of what was going on, and Harris was then pulled from the general population and transferred the following morning back to the prison farm near the town of Jones Creek. Within a couple of months, Michael Bouchee was paroled from prison and returned to Jefferson County, Texas. In fact, upon his release he moved into the family home of none other than his Brotherhood sponsor, Roland Harris.

Within two weeks, Bouchee reportedly got liquored up, and there inside the home of Harris' widowed mother, sexually assaulted Harris' sister, Linda Irene. Michael Bouchee would never be seen again. Rumor had it that he either became alligator bait in a Louisiana swamp, or he was cut up with a chain saw and fed to the crabs in a Gulf Coast salt water marsh. His death is a forgone conclusion, because he had never gone over a year during his adult life without being arrested.

The case went completely cold at this point. Linda Williams was never interviewed. She could never be linked with either the Aryan Brotherhood or Michael Bouchee.

You can't—and never will—win them all. In fact, every investigator knows they will, many times in a career, know who killed someone but never have enough evidence to convict or even indict them. Knowing who did something is one thing, but proving it to a group of people beyond a reasonable doubt is yet another.

•A BAJA, OKLAHOMA KILLING•

Dewey Pastor was a sixteen-year-old loser from Denison, Texas, which is located in the sector of northeast Texas up near the Oklahoma border. Baja, Oklahoma is what people from the Dallas-Fort Worth area call this region. It is as if the DFW (Dallas-Fort Worth, for you non-Texans) crowd does not want to acknowledge that this patch of dirt is really part of the state of Texas. Think of it as being like a down-at-the-heel relative you don't want people to know is in fact blood kin of yours. Pastor ran with a twenty-year-old mental midget named Ken Huska. Though he was not the sharpest knife in the drawer himself, Pastor was the obvious brains of the outfit.

We became acquainted with these two scholars after arresting both of them on murder warrants out of Grayson County.

Frank Scoggins and I walked into Homicide about 4 p.m. one Saturday afternoon, a little before our shift was to begin, and checked in with Joe Kunkle, the duty lieutenant. Joe, in his typical low-key manner, told us, "If you two Hon-yockers can break loose from whatever you're working on, I need you to get with some detectives with Denison PD. They had a couple of suspects charged in a murder from up there and they think they are in Houston working at a carnival." He gave us the names of the investigators we were to deal with and a phone number to call. We took it from there.

At this time in history it was an unwritten rule that you were to give any and all out-of-town cops every bit of assistance you could. This included driving them around, or in our case, trying to arrest and get confessions from wanted suspects. If fellow cops were in town for court because they'd arrested some crook of yours, you might drop them off at the better beer joints about seven and pour them into their motel room about eleven that evening. If you had a case where your suspect or witnesses were from out of town, you simply went around the squad room and asked if anyone knew a friendly investigator in say Phoenix, Los Angeles or Elephant's Ass, Nebraska. That was how business got taken care of. The Old Boy, or Good Old Boy, network is alive and works well in the business of law enforcement.

The north Texas cops advised us that they had a murder in their fair city where a fellow (who was a member of the indefinite sex) was shot and killed at an apartment demolition job site. It was a "there are no witnesses to this murder" kind of deal. Police learned about the murder when a city employee brought his daughter into the police station saying her former boyfriend called her the night before and told her about killing a "queer" at the apartment he was staying in at his job site. That young man was sixteen-year-old Dewey Pastor. He told the girl he and Ken Huska were leaving town until things cooled down and that they'd signed onto a carnival that was headed to Houston for a week. A check at the apartment at the job site did in fact reveal the dead man who had been shot to death.

The twenty-six-year-old dead man, Brady Portas, was reportedly a local pot head and a member of a wealthy Denison family. He reportedly had no criminal history. The killers in this case took not only their victim's life but his wallet and his car as well.

Pastor called the girl again from Houston, telling her that he ultimately was headed to Mexico to work in resorts. He figured the resorts could use English-speaking employees, and he had a semester of Spanish in school. The Denison cops asked that we go by a local carnival and see if the wanted guys were working there, and if so, arrest them and try and get statements from them.

The suspects had dumped the dead man's car in Centerville, Texas, in a parking lot where a carnival had been for a week. The Centerville police fingerprinted the car and were able to identify prints from both Dewey Pastor and Ken Huska inside and outside of the vehicle. The case had potential, but what it really needed was a good confession or two to cinch it down tight.

When we spoke to the Denison detectives we asked them which carnival their crooks were signed on with and where in Houston it was set up. They did not know, but it would be the only carnival in town. The small town cops were astounded to find out that Houston is over six hundred and sixty square miles inside the city limits, with another million people living in smaller towns and unincorporated suburbs around it. We said we would try and figure out how many carnivals were in town and go shoot those locations. We called our police dispatch office and had each of the patrol channels check to see if the street units knew of any carnivals set up in the city or just outside the city limits. We also called the Harris County Sheriff's Department and had them issue a general broadcast to their street units as to whether any carnivals were set up in their jurisdictions.

We came up with two that were set up in the city, and another in northeast Harris County. We got lucky—that number could have been much higher. We drove out to a carnival in shallow southwest Houston, in a largely Hispanic area off the Southwest Freeway and Windswept Lane. The cops call this area of town the Gulfton Ghetto. The carnival was set up near a big flea market, and had booths with games to win junk, a Ferris wheel and assorted rides. We walked up to the front entry gate, with guns on our hips and badges on our belts, and asked for the carnival bossman. He was pointed out to us and we asked about Dewey Pastor and Ken Huska. He said that yes, in fact, they had hired on in Centerville and were working at a nearby booth, so he walked us over to that booth and pointed them out. There was a big old hefty woman working the booth with them. She looked like she could have just stepped out of a Dickens novel. After the two north Texas boys were handcuffed the woman pointed out a backpack on a shelf behind where they'd been standing, saying it belonged to Dewey. It just so happened the murder weapon was inside that bag. Their gun was a stolen nine-shot Harrington & Richardson .22 revolver that loaded with CCI brand hollow points. Sometimes the fish really do jump into the boat. Then, sometimes you can't buy luck.

We transported both suspects to Homicide. They both gave rather self-serving statements, trying to justify their actions, at least in their own minds. After they'd signed statement one, we ran some facts past the idiots and they then gave second statements that probably came as close to the truth as either pinhead was able to. Pastor was a juvenile, so it was more work getting a judge to go over the statement with him outside the presence of any police officer. It worked out, though, and the gruesome dusome was locked up awaiting transport to the northern wastelands. The facts as they were laid out were such that it appeared Pastor got frustrated and just wanted to kill somebody that day.

Dewey Pastor was not in school at the time, because he'd dropped out. He was working for a construction company that had a contract to tear down a small, ratty apartment complex. A small, detached building that housed the laundromat and office sat just behind the single-story, ten-unit complex. Pastor had been living there for about a week prior to the murder. The old business office had electricity and a bathroom equipped with a shower. The air conditioner worked, and though not fancy, these accommodations worked for Pastor as a place to live away from his mother and stepdad.

Pastor particularly disliked his stepfather, James Lessor. It seems Lessor was as subtle as a brick in the side of the head and would tell Pastor that if he was too smart to stay in school, he should get off his lazy butt, get a job and act like a man. In fact, this whole murder episode began with Pastor wanting to lure his stepdad to his apartment so he could kill *him*. Pastor knew his stepdad was fond of good whiskey, so he called Lessor on the night he decided to try his hand at murder. He told Lessor he wanted to make amends and said he'd bought him a bottle of Makers Mark as a friendly gesture. James Lessor knew his wife's child was as worthless as a hope chest in a cathouse and said he was not interested. When Pastor tried to convince him he was trying to show good faith, Lessor told him to commit an anatomically impossible act and hung up the phone.

Following his encounter with Lessor, Pastor was furious and, according to Huska's second confession, was pacing back and forth in the cinderblock apartment saying he just wanted to kill somebody. Ken Huska hit on the idea of killing the most flaming gay blade in town, whose weakness was marijuana. Pastor called Brady Portas and told him that he and Ken Huska had come up with half a pound of hydroponically grown weed and they were trying to peddle it. He told Portas he would cut him in on a piece of the action if he could find buyers. Portas was offered the chance to sample the goods if he wanted to come over. Portas jumped at the chance to sample some really high-powered weed. When he arrived, Portas was immediately shot multiple times and was very likely dead soon after he hit the floor.

With a couple of pretty good confessions—taken after proper legal warning was administered by a magistrate—the north Texas murder was wrapped up pretty tightly. The Denison cops headed south and picked up their two wayward children, the murder weapon and four signed confessions. They were a bit astounded by the amount of work that we had done on their "queer killing." (It seems political correctness had not yet made its way to the northern regions of the state.)

They hauled their trash home and Frank Scoggins had an occasion to speak with one of the investigators a couple of months later. It seemed Dewey Pastor was trying to get himself certified to stand trial as an adult. The juvenile detention facility he was housed in would not let any of its underage detainees smoke tobacco there and the county jail allowed smoking in the exercise yard. Therefore, he'd directed his court-appointed attorney to try and get him certified as an adult as soon as possible so he could smoke a couple of times a day. His attorney had informed him that in his case a determinant sentence–one with a defined length that can't be changed by a parole board or other agency–was a real possibility. As a juvenile, Pastor might get a twenty-five or forty-year sentence, with the possibility of parole.

Once turning eighteen, Pastor would then be transferred to the adult department of corrections to serve the rest of his sentence in an adult prison. Pastor wanted to hurry his transition to living among adult criminals so he could smoke cigarettes for a few months longer.

You can't understand White Trash thought processes,

logic or priorities. So don't even try. You see, in reality, no tobacco of any kind is allowed inside Texas prisons. These folks are classified under an unofficial (police) classification of NHI, no human involvement. In the world of thinking people they could be organ donors at any given time because they are, for all intents and purposes, brain dead.

•FROM THE OTHER SIDE•

This story is not about a murder investigation, but an attempted murder. I will attest that it really occurred, though it is wild enough that it may come across as a story line made up by someone trying to crank out a made-for-TV script for a two-part series. It would have been a murder investigation had the intended victim not been fast on his feet. I wrote this for three reasons. First, it is to show how truly insane some people living among us really are. Second, to note that their perception of the world is every bit as strong to them as ours is to us. Third, if you don't record something like this it will be lost forever. This story is about people from two different worlds–worlds that differ markedly–and how sometimes those two universes collide.

Some years ago, a federal judge decided that people with severe mental disorders should no longer be detained in state-run mental institutions. As a result, mentally ill people who were once held in those places are now turned out onto the streets. Often their existence is meager at best. The mentally ill are cycled through the court system and there they get run into mental health testing for three to thirty days. After evaluations and medications to stabilize them, they are handed a bottle of pills and returned to the streets. When medicated, some of them are often quite tractable.

When they either run out of their meds, or simply stop taking them, the wheels come off the tracks. A train wreck will surely follow. Some of these folks can act quite normally while taking drugs that would make a rhino comatose.

Just because you work in a place called the Homicide Division does not mean every case you deal with has a murder attached to it. The investigator assigned to deal with the case in this story was named Jim Boy. That case involved a northeast Houston resident named Thad Lindsey, who was attacked by a neighbor brandishing a machete. Thad was taken to Ben Taub Hospital by ambulance and had two rather major wounds. The first was a chopping type wound to his left forearm–defensive wound that cut deadly into the bone. The second was a fairly deep cut to his right back, starting at the top of his shoulder and running approximately twelve inches downward. The wound to his back came about after he turned to flee from the machete-wielding mad man and was slashed as he ran.

Jim verified that Lindsey was still in the hospital and drove out to interview him. Lindsey said he knew the man who cut him and said the attack occurred without provocation. He said that the suspect was a crazy neighbor named Geraldo Towns who lived alone in what had been his family's home. Lindsey had known the suspect for maybe ten or fifteen years but stayed clear of him because he was not right in the head. Lindsey told Jim he was walking to work the day he was attacked. He was walking because the weather was nice and he only lived a couple of blocks from the tire store where he worked as an assistant manager.

Lindsey said up until two weeks prior he had not said so much as hello to Towns for a couple of years. On the day before the attack he was walking home from work and noticed–in Towns' yard–several little trees that were maybe four or five feet tall, that were bent over and staked to the ground. Lindsey thought it was really odd that each of the trees had a tag tied to it with some writing on the tags. He stopped to look at one of the tags and Towns came bolting out of his house, screaming and yelling for Lindsey to get off his property and told him to never walk down the street in front of his house again.

Lindsey said he just shook it off and figured there was really no benefit from arguing with a nut case, so he just walked on off. Then on the day of the attack, when he was walking down the street to work, Towns rushed up to him, let out a yell, and chopped at him with the machete. Lindsey threw up his arm to keep from getting cut on the neck or head, and as a result, his forearm took the brunt of the slash. The victim turned to run and was slashed on the back right shoulder as he fled. Lindsey said he was afraid to go home knowing the neighborhood crazy might come after him to finish the job.

Jim contacted Eugene Terry, who was listed in the offense report as a witness to the attack. Terry knew both parties involved in this case. He said Geraldo Towns had always been different while he was growing up, but since his mother died two years before, he'd gotten flat strange. Towns would sometimes walk around wearing some kind of crown on his head that he had woven out of grape vines, and either a loin cloth like Tarzan, or some bed sheet wrapped around his waist. Terry also said that Towns "talked all kinds of crazy stuff all the time" and everybody avoided him. The day before, Terry said, he had seen Thad Lindsey walking down the street and Geraldo Towns came out of his front door with a machete. Towns ran up to Lindsey and gave some kind of yell before he tried to chop Lindsey in the neck or head. Lindsey threw up an arm and got hacked in the forearm before he turned and ran. Towns struck at Lindsey again as he turned and ran, but Terry did not know if he'd connected with the second cut of the big knife.

With the information he'd gathered from the interviews, Jim headed for the Harris County District Attorney's Intake Section. Upon review, a charge of aggravated assault with a deadly weapon was filed. The warrant was filed first with the District Clerk and then Jim took the paperwork to the District Court of authority and the warrant was signed and made valid.

Every sector of Houston has a police tactical unit made up of tough and aggressive street officers who do follow-up investigations, execute warrants and basically harangue crooks. They also stake out locations and hunt fugitives. Those officers were put into that unit because of their knowledge of the system and due to the fact they are workers and hustlers. Jim contacted the Tactical unit for the part of town the crook lived in. Their unit supervisor jumped at the chance to put another crook into the iron house. He said that warrant execution was something his troops lived for. Jim went with them because it was his case and he wanted to be part of it from start to finish. Geraldo Towns answered their knock at his door and was arrested without incident. It was noted that when he came to the door, Towns was wearing his crown of woven branches and there was a cone of incense imbedded in one branch and that it was still smoking. He was also carrying a four-foot-long carved wooden staff. When told of the warrant he said he understood because he was a Treasury agent. Jim started visiting with Towns and the two men got along well enough.

As their conversation progressed, Jim got a bit of an insight into how his prisoner's mind worked—or maybe didn't work. When asked about how he became a Treasury agent, Towns said that they (the Treasury Department) began sending him checks so he figured they'd hired him to do the job. In actuality, his aunt had signed him up for social security disability benefits because of his mental issues and that was why Towns was receiving checks from the Treasury Department. Towns took on the role of tour guide and went in depth, trying to explain to Jim how things were in his world. Towns said that there were only five places on the continent of North America where people were able to be reincarnated back into powerful North American Indians who had once ruled this portion of the globe. Towns just happened to live in one of those five locations.

Inside Towns' home, there was a four-foot-wide picture on a wall in the front room that was very stark. It had been done in either chalk or pastels on canvas. There were three ghostly persons pictured (a woman and a preteen boy and girl) that were sort of washed-out or gray-tinged black people. The background had trees with black gnarled branches that were devoid of leaves. A few dark, wispy clouds were seen against a leaden grey sky. The expressions of the three people were somber and their large sad eyes seemed to follow you as you moved around the room. Jim asked about the picture and was told, "That is my family—on the other side." Jim Boy said the picture was haunting, and that in some social circles he could see some of the artsy crowd paying big bucks for a framed and matted version of such a thing.

Towns then went into the trees that he had staked down around the property. He explained that they were "bow units" as he called them, and were actually long bows in the making. He went on to say that he was producing bows and gold bullion as a future income source. Each of the trees, or bow units, was tagged and assigned a serial number, and had been cataloged in a ledger book he kept. Towns obviously knew nothing of woods, as Chinese tallow trees are pithy and fast-growing but would become very brittle once they were cut and fashioned into bows.

His gold bullion manufacturing operation was a really whacked-out concept that was even harder to grasp. Towns explained that due to his reincarnation, he had been blessed with the knowledge of being able to turn his "Guano," or dung, into gold bullion by aging it for a year while it was encased in plastic bags. These bags he kept stored in his bathtub. He specifically had to "harvest" his dung during the dark of the moon and as close to midnight as he possibly could.

Jim's suspect was matter-of-fact as to the reason for his attack on his neighbor. Towns said that he had caught Thad Lindsey trespassing on his property several weeks before and had seen him examining and touching one of his bow units. Towns said he warned Lindsey not to walk down the street in front of his house ever again. What's more, it was very obvious that Towns felt quite justified in his actions. "After all—he'd been warned." While searching the bullion and bow tree factory, one of the uniformed officers found a bag of marijuana. When the blue suit showed it to Jim Boy, their suspect blurted out, "Yes I smoke ganja, but some of us use it as a sacrament, you know."

The suspect was transported from the scene and taken to the city jail for fingerprints and photos before being transferred to the county jail. To this day, Jim Boy keeps an 8 x 12 photograph of himself wearing Towns' grapevine crown and holding the crazy's hand-carved wooden staff.

Welcome to a view of the other side. Hopefully you will never have the occasion to meet with any of the folks that live there. It appears theirs may well be a land of no return.

•A REAL LADY KILLER•

Karl Wilson had a history of violence toward girls and women, going back to his teens. He was not overly bright and barely made it out of high school, and then, only because his mother tutored him nightly. Wilson excelled at only one thing in school–sports. He was aggressive and explosive on the football field and in the boxing ring. He hit hard and fast.

When he was fifteen he attacked a woman and beat her down. She was a stranger to him; the two had never met before. Wilson was walking his after-school paper route and went to the woman's door and knocked. When she opened the door, he attacked and beat her unconscious. He then finished throwing his papers and returned home for the evening. Wilson was identified by the victim, and arrested. Since he was only fifteen, he went into the juvenile system and finally into an outpatient mental health treatment program. His records showed he had an antisocial personality and that he dreamed of attacking women. He claimed he enjoyed the dreams, in which women were either beaten or stabbed. School records indicated Wilson had been reprimanded several times for minor assaults on several girls he was in classes with.

I did not work any of the Texas cases involving Wilson.

At the time he began killing, I was investigating armed robberies. Wilson was an unknown in Houston's police files before his first arrest. He killed ten women in Houston that we know of, all because "They were evil." He was a stalker in the purest and truest since of the word. This killer was only moderately organized, and a bit of an opportunist. Once our paths crossed and I studied him, the excitement and glee he experienced was what astounded me most.

I transferred into Homicide about a year after he pled guilty to attempted murder and worked with some of the men who dealt with him. Wilson was a hands-on killer–physically very strong and liked to use either a knife or his hands when he attacked his victims. He did not stick with the same program in each attack, but was an urban hunter and stalker. His victims were people he'd simply just happened upon and followed. Ten women were slain by him in Houston in a twelve-month period. One victim was a jogger he killed and whose body he left hanging in a tree near a university campus. He drowned another victim in an apartment swimming pool. Some were cut with knives, and others strangled. The only planning he did was to ensure that he did not leave evidence behind. Wilson explained to one investigator that he wore rubber gloves to never leave behind fingerprints. He wore hoodie-type T-shirts or sweat shirts with the strings pulled tight to keep him from losing hair during any struggle. When he hunted, he simply drove around looking for a lone female that interested him, then he would follow her.

Three of the women's bodies in our jurisdiction were hidden in culverts or buried, and Wilson eventually led our troops to the locations of their remains. While driving to one location, officers drove past a woman on a bicycle. The shackled prisoner looked at her and said, "She's evil.

If I weren't with you guys I'd follow her." The woman he pointed out was a white female with dark hair. All but one of his victims I know of were white females, and all but two of those had dark hair. Only one victim was black. Before Wilson came to Texas there were a couple of survivors among his multiple attack victims. Two of those ladies claimed he was obviously so thrilled with his attacks that he laughed and jabbered like a child pumped up on sugar at a birthday party. Neither victim, however, could positively identify him.

Wilson did not live in Houston or Harris County, but resided seventy miles west of downtown Houston. He would drive into the city to do his hunting, and then return to small town life where he worked quietly, doing mechanical repairs for an oil company.

Our killer liked to attack women at night, typically late Saturday nights or early Sunday mornings. In a northern city he was called The Sunday Morning Slasher. That seemed to be his only real pattern. When arrested, he had followed a dark-headed white female named Katy Jantz home on a Saturday night and attacked her as she was opening her second-story apartment door. He choked her unconscious with his hands and dragged her limp body into her apartment. Her roommate was awake and came in to see a smiling Karl Wilson cross their threshold as he pulled Katy inside by her arms. Wilson struck like a snake and grabbed the roommate, Margie Koll, by the neck and attempted to choke the life from her too. Margie knew at once she could not break free from Wilson, so after a short struggle she went limp and collapsed, faking that she had passed out. He half carried-half dragged her into a bedroom, threw her on a bed and bound her hands behind her back with coat hangers from the closet. Margie later told police that after he bound her hands Wilson was so excited he literally jumped up and down, clapping his hands and giggling. After securing Margie, Wilson returned to Katy Jantz and dragged her into the bathroom and turned on the water in the tub. As the water was running, Margie got up and opened the sliding glass door leading out onto a concrete landing which overlooked a courtyard. She threw herself over the railing and hit the ground screaming. She continued to scream for help until neighbors came out to check on her and called 911.

One neighbor ran to the women's apartment and found the suspect gone. Katy Jantz was face down in the bathtub water and not breathing. That neighbor had been a lifeguard in his teens and immediately began administering CPR. Soon, Katy gagged and choked, and began breathing on her own. Patrol units responded immediately and Wilson was located at the back of the property, hiding behind a dumpster. Margie Koll made a positive identification of Wilson, and he was subsequently jailed and charged with both aggravated assault and attempted murder. He went through the system and was appointed an attorney within a couple of days.

That attorney of record approached the chief prosecutor of the court with a wild story and proposition. He told the prosecutor that his client was a serial killer, and had killed ten women in Houston. It was obvious that the defense wanted to get his client off the street, but also knew his law license would be in jeopardy if he did not provide an adequate defense. After some discussion, the attorney and the chief prosecutor settled on Wilson pleading guilty to an attempted murder charge and the court meeting out a sixty-year sentence. In exchange for his guilty plea, the state would agree not to prosecute Wilson for any of the murders he committed in Harris County, Texas. Off the record, the defense attorney said the police in all previous locations where Wilson had lived should check their uncleared murders, particularly where manual strangulation and knives were involved. Their combined hope was that Wilson would never step outside a prison setting alive. The best laid plans don't always work out.

The agreement was struck and Wilson told the cops about all of his killings in Houston. Three were only missing person cases until he led police to the bodies. The jogger left hanging in a tree had been strangled with the knitted scarf she wore around her neck. Given the way Wilson hung her body, the woman's death had been written off as a suicide, blamed on the stress of mid-term exams. The drowning at an apartment swimming pool had been ruled an accidental death where a woman came home after a few drinks at a night club and fell into the swimming pool.

During interviews with Wilson, he refused talk about any other cases he had been involved in. On one occasion, however, he did say that the number of women he'd murdered numbered around eighty. He understood talking about any killings outside of Houston could lead to more convictions, or a possible death penalty. Wilson pled guilty on his attempted murder charge after a written contract was made. The judge in the case, however, screwed up royally. When issuing his sentence, the judge failed to read into the record that the defendant used means that were considered to be a deadly weapon, namely the water in the tub where he attempted to kill Katy Jantz. This error meant the suspect did not have to serve two-thirds of his sentence before being eligible for parole.

Wilson was a model prisoner and without the deadly weapon stipulation, he was able to qualify for parole after doing a quarter of his sentence. He was earning time off of his sentence at the rate of three days extra for every one he served. When the ten-year mark was close, everybody scrambled to find another case in another jurisdiction for which Wilson might be prosecuted. Investigators knew Wilson had lived for a time in Michigan, and they were able to link him to a case there by fingerprints. Wilson was convicted in that case and sentenced to a long hitch in the Michigan prison system. Justice smiled, and within three years of his Michigan confinement, Wilson died of cancer. While in prison he'd made the comment that if released, he would kill again.

Wilson's killings were not sexual in nature–it was the act of killing he reveled in. There was no evidence of sexual assault in any of his known cases. In fact, his ex-wife said that during their short-term marriage, that after having sex, Carl would go for long walks and return in a sullen mood.

Author's note:

I attended undergraduate and graduate school, earning degrees in police administration. Textbooks and "criminologists" carry on, claiming that most serial killers are white males. While working in Homicide for a couple of decades in America's fourth largest city, I personally worked on two serial killers. Both were black. One of those two had been a serial rapist who always brutally beat his elderly white victims. Then he moved on to beating them to death. We cleared that case through DNA. That gentleman had been charged with murder in Arkansas. He had two trials, each ending in hung juries. The Arkansas district attorney worked out a deal with that killer. They told him they would not retry his case if he permanently moved out of state. That's how he ended up in Texas, where he worked as an unarmed security guard. Some members of this population of killers are police buffs and study investigative practices and procedures. All I could ever figure was that they operate under the "know your enemy" premise.

I did not work on Carl Wilson's case. During my tenure

in Houston PD Homicide, I recall five know serial killers–three black, one Hispanic and one Caucasian. Maybe I'm not the right kind of number cruncher–I've always been more a student of human behavior. I think, however, that many people who are bean counters or academicians do not report these crime statistics correctly, for fear of being called a racist. Who in their right mind cares about what color a mad dog is before you either cage it or kill it?

Either the gutless among us, or those pinheads with a politically correct obsession, that's who.

•MEXICO RANCH JUSTICE•

The names of all persons here and the locations in this story have been changed. The events are true but the state in which it occurred may or may not be correct. I may well be the only person alive that knows what really happened that day, and for me not share it would be a shame. I have spent time in Mexico's interior as well as on border ranches, where life for many is still very primitive and hardscrabble. Also the word of any ranch Patron is more than just the law of the land.

I can tell this story because the man who lived it and relayed it to me is no longer living. Though he is gone I will not use his real name, thereby not forsaking the trust he placed in me.

Lester Callaghan was a tall, lean man who served as a border patrolman for around three and a half decades. He worked much of it in the west Texas/Trans Pecos-Mexico border country. He began his career there in the later 1950s when radio contact was spotty on its best day in the high desert area known as the Big Bend country. Horses and open top Jeeps were often the best means of transportation in the rough areas. Moreover, at that time, patrol vehicles and trucks were not air conditioned. The border agents' main goal was to locate and detain illegal aliens for the purpose of deportation. In those days, agents did not work under the current administration's "catch and release" program that present day border agents must comply with. Border patrolmen never knew if they were coming up on humans looking for ranch work, human traffickers, contrabandistas, or fugitives from justice from either side of the Rio Grande. They just handled whatever they came upon—or, as Les told me, "You saddled your own broncs."

At the time of this story, there had been a rash of burglaries and thefts from ranch houses and outbuildings in close proximity to the river, as well as from area hunting camps. Thieves were carrying off guns, saddles and tack, as well as items that were small and easily portable. Based on footprints left behind it appeared two crooks came afoot and would maybe carry off a saddle apiece. Only footprints were found—no tire tracks. It was as if the suspects likely used either backpacks or cloth feed sacks for the smaller items they stole. Burlap feed sacks (called croaker sacks) were favored by the illegal walkers because they would sew up both ends of the sack and cut a slit in its middle so they could load it through the hole in the middle and walk off wearing the "saco" like a poncho. Their load was carried in both front and back and was better balanced for foot travel. The crooks particularly liked to carry off long guns and saddles, though they would never pass up a handgun. West Texans all kept guns around as a matter of necessity. The ladrones (thieves) might stake out a hunting camp and sneak in at night and steal a few guns after the hunters had gone to bed. By the time their theft was discovered in the early morning hours, the crooks were either headed back to, or already inside, Mexico.

Early one morning, Les was doing a horseback sweep along the river near the Black Gap Wildlife Management

Area, which sits not far from Big Bend National Park. He was looking for evidence of heavy crossing sights—for either humans or livestock—that would indicate aliens were bypassing the official checkpoints. It was early April, and the weather was pleasant and the earth was coming alive after a cold winter. Les stopped in the Black Gap headquarters a little after eight that morning figuring the coffee would have finished perking about then. One of the maintenance workers came in cussing that somebody had stolen two saddles and some farrier tools from the saddle shed overnight. Les went outside and saw the tracks of two men leading away from the outbuilding and headed toward the Rio Grande River. He followed the tracks on horseback, making good time since the two folks in question had obviously made no attempt to hide their trail. Tracking from horseback was something he was well versed in, as most all border agents track humans regularly and still have the reputation for being exceptional rough country man trackers.

The tracks led Les to a fishing camp on the American side of the river and the men there reported that one of them had an expensive scoped rifle that had been stolen overnight from a canoe he'd beached at the river's edge. The suspects' tracks then meandered upstream for a couple hundred yards from the camp, and then crossed the river onto a ranch owned by the Marquez family.

Don Francisco Marquez was the Patron of that ranch and he ran cattle on the American side of the river as well. He had the grazing rights leased on all the Black Gap Wildlife Management Area as well as some adjoining multi-section ranches. A section of land amounts to 640 acres, or a square mile. Because of the harsh desert terrain, it takes a lot of acreage per cow, sheep or goat to graze livestock in that ranch country.

Les could see the tracks went into Marquez's land and were visible in the loose sand going up a canyon. Les opted to return to the Black Gap headquarters and agency staff members were able to reach Mr. Marquez by telephone. Mr. Marquez asked that Les Callaghan bring his horse and meet him at the fishing camp in three hours' time. The lawman had time for a couple of cups of coffee, his horse got some oats, and they headed back to the river.

Don Francisco Marquez arrived at the appointed time, also on horseback, and in the company of two very tough looking vaqueros. The man whose rifle had been stolen was still present and he and Marquez were already well acquainted as they had done several livestock business deals over the years. Marquez and each of his vaqueros were armed both with revolvers and lever-action rifles. Marquez requested that the border patrolman accompany them onto his ranch in search of the thieves. Les agreed and they tracked the two men about two and a half miles into the ranch. The footprints led to a dirt-floored line shack. Les told me that you really needed to give the structure a promotion to even call it a shack. He was always amazed at the conditions under which the peon class lived, working for a beans-and-tortillas existence, and little more.

Upon arriving at the shack, they encountered two laborers employed by the ranch. Marquez advised them that he and the United States official had tracked two thieves from the Rio Grande (called the Rio Bravo on the Mexican side) to their shack. The men denied leaving the ranch or knowing anyone involved in any thefts. They said nobody had come there overnight or that day. Marquez ordered his vaqueros to tie up the peon laborers both hand and foot. The two men were thrown to the ground (more likely knocked to the ground) and trussed up. One of the vaqueros searched the shack and found nothing of value except a new enameled coffee pot. The other vaquero then went to his horse and retrieved a cattle prod from a burlap bag he had tied onto the back of his saddle.

Marquez asked his vaqueros if the tracks they'd followed were made by the two laborers and they said they were. These vaqueros were "Hombres de Campos"—men skilled in tracking humans and animals, riding, roping, and shooting. They were part of an upper caste of ranch laborer in the rural, almost feudal, society of ranch life. Many of the ranch peons were born onto the ranches, worked and were buried there at the end of their lives. After an extended application, or session, of electric shock therapy the peons admitted to the theft and being the ones who had been robbing the ranch houses and hunting camps along the river. They said they had buried the saddles and rifle and were planning to sell them to men on area ranchos as they had in the past. (Mexicans very often preferred American roping saddles if they could afford them, because Mexican rigs were often made with green wooden saddle trees that were wrapped in raw buckskin, and were inferior to American made saddles.) The captives claimed they kept nothing from their thefts as they wanted nothing to be able to link them to their crimes.

The laborers were forced to dig up the stolen items and after doing so, Marquez had their hands rebound behind their backs and had them positioned on their knees. Then, with only a nod to his cowboys, the vaqueros drew their revolvers and shot both men once time each in the center of their backs. Marquez then walked over to where the bodies lay and fired a round into each of the cadavers. He turned to Les Callaghan and said, in Spanish, "Now Mister Border Patrolman it is time for you to shoot each of these men also. This way we will all be equally guilty of murder and will not later feel remorse about what happened here today. What's more we do not have to worry about anyone bringing someone else legal problems at some later date."

Les did as he was directed. He said the thought that came into his head immediately after being told this by the Patron was, "Who am I to argue with three armed men in a foreign country where nobody knows where the hell I am?"

Marquez had his cowboys go back to the brush corral behind the line shack and bring around the two burros that were penned there. The donkeys were produced, with pack saddles on their backs and the stolen items lashed to them. Les was asked to bring the animals and their packs back to the ranch and just leave the pack saddles one hundred yards north of the river and up the canyon where they had tracked the thieves. Marquez said to just turn the burros loose on the Mexican side and they would find their way home all by themselves. After giving Les instructions, the Patron turned his vaqueros and told them in Spanish, "Dispose of these two (as he pointed to the newly rehabilitated thieves) so that not even the coyotes will ever find them." They answered as one, saying "Si Patron" and shook out their catch ropes to drag off the carcasses.

Lester Callaghan's official report was filed the next morning. He documented how the ranch owner on the Mexican side of the border and his men tracked the two suspects a couple of miles into the ranch and found the stolen goods that had been hidden off in some brush beside the game trail they were following. The tracks of the suspects were lost where they'd crossed a rocky ledge and headed toward a ridge. It further read that two unknown and unnamed ranch hands brought all of the stolen property to the international border and turned it over to Callaghan there at the river. The suspects' identities and location remained unknown.

During this time in history it was common for United States lawmen to cross into Mexico, armed, while dealing with Mexican officials. Wanted suspects were regularly handed over to American police at the international bridges after bounties of a few hundred dollars were paid. Today, if United States lawman entering Mexico were armed, it would be considered an armed invasion. Les' era was a simpler and less complex time. On this one occasion a matter was handled quickly in the Land of Manyana. Similarly when this sort of justice is meted out, the recidivism rate (suspects returning to a life of crime) is quite low.

As an aside, I am sure that the word got around among the peons on El Rancho Marquez that it would be best not to follow the path of *los dos ladrones*. In Mexico they have a saying for just about everything. The one that seems most appropriate here is, "Los muertos no hablen" which, translated, means "The dead don't talk."

The practice of everyone being equally guilty of murder is not unique to Mexico and men like Don Francisco Marquez. When I was in my late teens, I was told by old folks in central Texas of two occasions when this same practice was carried out. The admitted killers were in Austin County, near the city of Bellville and again in New Braunfels, near San Antonio. If there was someone in the area badly misbehaving—such as a thief, a rapist or the like, a group of men would get together, grab the wayward soul and carry him off. They would dump him off by a roadside, or along a river or stream, and each of them would shoot him in the body with their shotguns. They did not shoot the subject of their attention in the face in case the family might want an open coffin viewing. The reason they did this was out of respect for the dead man's family. Because, I was told, some evil doers come from good families. A point in question being that John Wesley Hardin was the son of a Methodist preacher from Evergreen, Texas. He was named after a man of the cloth, but instead of reading to others from the good book he sent a large number of men to be read over before they were laid to rest.

Again, the logic was that the participants were all equally guilty of murder and if one of the guilty parties told on another, they would be incriminating themselves also. From what I gathered it may have been an old country practice. Who knows.

Les never told anyone he worked with about the killing of the border thieves. Just why he trusted me with the information I am not sure. Les promoted up the ranks of his organization and retired as a captain. A couple of years before his retirement the border patrol brought horses back into field use. Then Captain Callaghan decided one day to go out on horse patrol with his troops about a month before he was slated to retire. He was issued a mount named Spook that day. Spook was a long-legged black gelding and Les wondered if it was named as some sort of a racist comment. It didn't take long to figure out that the animal got his name because he had vision problems and spooked at all manner of things while being ridden. Anyway, while taking his horseback trip down memory lane Les Callaghan rode up to a regular crossing place just north of Eagle Pass, Texas. The border patrolmen watched a group of twelve illegals cross into Los Estados Unidos. Caught up with his young troops' excitement, Les thundered up on the "walkers" when they were fifty yards into the country. Spook slid to a stop and one of the Mexicans threw his hands up the air as if to proclaim he was surrendering.

That was all the horse needed. He began pitching and bucking like a good rodeo saddle bronc horse. Les lost his handheld radio first and his pistol went another direction before he too was bounced off the animal. As the dusty captain and leader of men was getting up and gathering up his equipment, one of the illegals came up to him, leading his mount. As he handed the reins to Les, the peon laborer told him in Spanish, "You did not have to get off of your horse mister—we were not going to run from you." The other illegals—along with Les' subordinates—had a good laugh over that one. For that matter, so did Les' wife. Twenty-five-odd years later, *that* story is still being told.

•ABOUT THE AUTHOR•

Sgt. Brian Foster spent thirty-four years in law enforcement, twenty-three of those in the Houston Police Department's Homicide Division where he personally made twenty-five to thirty-eight murder scenes a year, on average.

Brian now lives in an undisclosed location in Texas with his wife and dogs, and between chores "around the place" he is hard at work on the next book in the Texas True Crime series.

You can reach Brian through his website www.texastruecrime.com.

•FROM THE AUTHOR•

There are now seven generations of Fosters who have made their homes in Texas. They first came here when Texas was a part of northern Mexico and the Mexicans wanted a group of Anglos to serve as a buffer against raiding Comanches from the high plains.

By lying and claiming to be Catholic, the early Fosters were able to secure a land grant in what is now part of Austin and Washington counties, along the Brazos River. My ancestors participated in the revolution of the Texians against the Mexican army, and one family member was captured as a prisoner of war, along with James Walker Fannin, following the Battle of Goliad. That Foster ancestor was murdered by a firing squad at the mission of La Bahia. The murdered man's father, already in his seventies, orchestrated part of what came to be known as The Runaway Scrape from Austin County, directing the escape of women and children from the advancing Mexican army.

My great-grandfather was asked to resign from the office of sheriff of Austin County after he shot and killed three men in front of the county courthouse for "back-talking" him. His actions were deemed too outlandish for an elected official. He was not, however, indicted for murder because the three men he killed that day were all trash and the world was a better place without them. His son, my grandfather, fled to Houston as a fugitive from justice following a shooting near the Washington and Waller county line. He went on to become a wealthy man, but never returned to Austin County, Texas.

The members of my tribe still tend to have rough ways, and often speak their minds before thinking. There's no doubt my family history prepared me well for a career in homicide; in fact, some might argue it was my destiny. And while many of the men (and women) I worked with through my years in law enforcement also had rough ways, many of them were some of the most upstanding and hard-working people I've ever known.

The world is a better—and safer—place because of them.

CPSIA information can be obtained
at www.ICGtesting.com
Printed in the USA
FFOW04n1409250116
20807FF